IIE Research Report Number Twenty-Six

talking to themselves

THE SEARCH FOR RIGHTS AND RESPONSIBILITIES OF THE PRESS AND MASS MEDIA IN FOUR LATIN AMERICAN NATIONS

CRAUFURD D. GOODWIN, Duke University
MICHAEL NACHT, University of Maryland

Institute of International Education

IIE gratefully acknowledges support from the Ford Foundation for this research report. The views expressed herein are those of the authors and not necessarily shared by IIE or the Ford Foundation.

Contents

Foreword

The recent advance of democracy in several areas of the globe has opened crucial opportunities for freedom of the press. Yet the demise of authoritarian systems does not guarantee what *quality* of free press may emerge. In Latin America, and in Eastern Europe as well, hundreds of new newspapers and magazines are all increasingly testing the waters of freedom. Too many, however, have brought old vices into a new reality. Only a handful here and there have made honest, persistent, and committed efforts to build media that are high-quality, analytical, and independent. Too many remain overly devoted to advocating political beliefs, portraying issues in stark black-and-white, or taking one party's views as godsend or another's as evil—without the slightest regard for deeper concerns.

People used to a high-quality free press generally take its benefits for granted. In fact, when thinking of the media they tend to project an ideal, even a utopian model of their own reality—and vociferously condemn any perceived infringement of it, however small. Most societies that have invested the past several centuries building and experiencing democracy have probably spent much of the same interval watching how the media evolve and conform to the demands of the democratic process. Rules and regulations, practices and norms, and ethical considerations have all been accumulating over the centuries to bring about a truly independent, analytical, responsible, and thus reliable free press.

In countries that are just emerging from years or decades, if not centuries, of authoritarian rule, the media may seem just one more component of a complex process that will gradually shape itself. But as this book convincingly argues, the nature and future of the media ought to be addressed as an issue in its own right. There are no simple or, more importantly, single answers for key questions about ownership, competition, government subsidies and advertising, journalists' rights and responsibilities, and so on. These are not merely academic questions: they have to do with whether citizens can make informed judgments on the very issues that democracy has made possible.

Without media that cater to the information needs of the citizenry, democracy ends up a mockery of what it could otherwise be. Citizens need information, analyses, and opinions if they are to be able to decide for themselves—to discern, as the authors of this book put it, their own self-interests in a complex new environment.

That is why it is imperative to analyze and assess the evolution, challenges, and potential of the media in emerging democracies. And that is why this is an important book, on an important, indeed crucial, subject. It is also a smart book, for its authors do not pretend to settle all debate about the press in Latin America. In fact they deliberately pose many more questions than a single book can reasonably offer answers to. What this book does extremely well, instead, is to develop a framework through which any reader can recognize and consider the complexity of the challenges that confront the Latin American media today—most particularly in the countries featured in discussion but also in other countries throughout the hemisphere that share the experience of moving toward a democratic polity.

As this book constantly portrays, these challenges are neither small nor easily surmounted. How does one develop a free press? Can anyone come up with prescriptions for such an endeavor? Should an American model be adopted (or adapted)? A European model? Can or should a new and really different paradigm be attempted? The authors state their own ideas and make some specific recommendations. But the larger value of the book is in how it applies concepts to specific countries in Latin America—and in the thinking the reader is forced to do as a result. None of the issues raised about the media are easy ones. But the reader will emerge with a firm notion of what those issues are and what difficulties must be met.

The underlying focus of this book is on what the role of the media in a free society can and should be. Although the reader gets a picture of how the media operate in the four countries the authors surveyed, and the distinctive opportunities and constraints at work in each, discussion does not dwell overlong on how things got to be the way they presently are. Two more timely factors are never far from immediate view: the people, whose needs and interests the media should attend to; and the role of government in the development of healthy, competitive media.

It should be obvious that the center of gravity in a democracy is the individual citizen. The entire purpose of the media should be to serve the needs of such individuals by providing information (facts), analysis, opinion, investigation, and entertainment. But what if the individual does not know how to discern facts from opinions? What if the individual has lived so long under an authoritarian regime that he (or she) cannot accept plain facts as better than tainted opinions? These are not irrelevant issues in societies that have not known civic freedom for a long time.

Although the educational system will have to bear the long-term responsibility for developing free and responsible citizens, only the media can fill these short- and medium-term needs in emerging democracies. This in turn presents a very basic dilemma: citizens cannot demand from the media what they do not know they want, or at least cannot very exactly identify; nor can the media offer material that their various audiences do not demand. Only truly enlightened media—and note that the authors consistently treat the word as plural, denoting diversity in commonality—can break out of this vicious cycle.

And the risk is worse than at first meets the eye: to the extent that only the wealthy demand "clean" media, nobody else will get any such thing—with ominous consequences for economic development, for equitable distribution of income, and for democracy. Most Latin American nations have long been characterized not only by some variety of authoritarian government but by an extremely skewed distribution of wealth as well as of all goods and services, including education, health services, physical infrastructure, and so forth. If those who have historically benefited from economic development end up becoming the only citizens who can easily advocate their own interests and influence the future, the whole point of democracy will have been lost. A free press is a necessary condition for democracy to thrive. But clearly it is not a sufficient one.

Governments face a dilemma of their own. Most governments the world over would much rather control the media than cater to it. But most governments of democratic nations have come to accept and respect the role that the media play in democracy, even while trying to restrict the media's access to various areas of government, such as "state secrets" or the private lives of government officials. In emerging democracies, however, governments are often so absorbed in other pressing issues of governance that they would prefer simply to control or—better still—ignore the media. To restate my earlier point a little differently: it would take a truly enlightened government to foster the development of media that could serve the needs of citizens who may not not know, or cannot yet articulate, what they desire from their newly democratic society.

A democracy can hardly prosper without independent and objective media that see the individual citizen as the ultimate target audience. To those who already enjoy such a privilege in long-established democracies, some of the points made here may at first seem elementary, even ludicrously obvious. But to those of us who do not, they are fresh issues of paramount importance. The reader of this book will certainly learn why.

Luís Rubio
Director General
CIDAC—Centro de Investigacion para el Desarrollo A.C.

Preface

The project that led to this monograph is part of the Institute of International Education's policy research program, initiated by IIE President Richard Krasno and its former Research Director, Elinor Barber, and directed by IIE Vice President Peggy Blumenthal. We have contributed earlier studies to that program dealing with, respectively, U.S. policies toward foreign students, the effects of an American education on foreign alumni, ways of sustaining the fruits of American higher education after students return home, and the increasing popularity of study abroad among American students.

The original vision for this study came from Thomas Trebat, then Regional Director for Latin America and the Caribbean at the Ford Foundation. We are grateful to the Ford Foundation for supporting the project through a grant to the Institute for International Education and to the staff of the Foundation in the Latin American region for facilitating the field work, especially Norman Collins, Representative for Mexico and the Caribbean, Joan Dassin, then Representative in Brazil, and Ramón Daubón, then Representative for the Andes and the Southern Cone. During 1992 and 1993 we paid visits to Argentina, Brazil, Chile, and Mexico and in a relatively short time held interviews with a wide range of persons well informed about the press and mass media. We were assisted with great efficiency by a resident of each of the countries we visited: Alberto Diaz-Cayeros in Mexico, Louise Byrne in Brazil, Leslie Crawford in Chile, and Patricia Vasquez in Argentina. Beth Eastlick and Vanessa Spann managed the details of the project from Durham, North Carolina with their characteristic skill and good humor. Laura Oaks gave the manuscript polish that it originally lacked.

Above all, we express our profound appreciation to all those journalists, public figures, scholars, and others who gave freely of their time to us in both Americas. This essay is based substantially on their conversations, and unquestionably it could not have been brought to conclusion without their full cooperation. We entered this project persuaded that free and effective press and mass media are central to the health of a liberal democracy, a market economy, and a free society. We emerged absolutely convinced that this is indeed the case. We shall feel our efforts have been fully worthwhile if this study contributes to the strengthening of Latin American media in any small way. We hope in particular that our observations and speculations may stimulate others in both hemispheres to pursue in depth a topic that we were able only to explore in outline. They will discover a wealth of interesting questions.

Several friends kindly read a preliminary version of this manuscript, saving us from numerous errors and misrepresentations, but bearing no responsibility in consequence for those that remain. We thank especially Peggy Blumenthal, Bryna Brennan, Alberto Diaz-Cayeros, Jorge Castenada, George Krimsky, Luís Rubio, Tom Trebat, and Chris Welna. We also benefitted from the views of various journalism training providers and donors, expressed during a meeting convened at IIE in May, 1994 to review this report in manuscript form. Their comments and ideas regarding future training needs are summarized in the appendix to this report.

Introduction

The distinguished American journalist Charles Kuralt recently remarked that in the press "you can hear a nation talking to itself."[1] He spoke of "wonderful voices" that lead to "a healthy accommodation of our differences," to equality and inclusion, and to the building of a fair society—referring to the United States. This essay grew out of listening to four other nations talking to themselves. It deals with what these conversations mean to these nations and to their neighbors in the United States to the north.

In the years since World War II, after the end of conventional empires, the industrialized world has become accustomed to giving development assistance to the less developed countries of the "South." Typically this assistance has consisted of capital goods, technology, training, and advice concerning institutional change. Over the last decade or so one of the most important aspects of the development process has been a transition of many such countries to democracy and a free market system, especially in Latin America but also in selected parts of Africa and Asia. The democratization process has spread, of course, to Central and Eastern Europe and to the republics of the former Soviet Union as well. To assist this process the more advanced countries have shifted their attention somewhat from the technical features of economic development to the less easily specified transformation of social and political institutions. They have offered advice and assistance in the establishment and reform of legislatures, legal systems, market structures, and both public and private devices to constrain and strengthen liberal economic and political processes.

One dimension of this transformation that has been relatively neglected by the emerging liberal democracies and those who would assist them is the set of mechanisms whereby the members of a free society come to understand and to have a voice in shaping the social change all around them. There are several reasons why these mechanisms are important. For most of the population they are the only means whereby a reasoned basis may be discovered for the vote and for support of one political party, faction, or leader over another. Unfiltered testimony from politicians alone tends to portray issues in stark black or white when in reality they are usually variable shades of gray. During periods of rapid change, these mechanisms are also the only means for citizens to gain balanced understanding of novel relationships and experiences. This understanding is important so that citizens can answer questions reasonably for themselves and thereby discern their own self-interest in a complex new environment.

The following are examples of questions citizens are likely to face in all the countries in transition: Is the division of powers among the executive, legislative, and judicial branches just and working effectively? Are fluctuating prices an indication of selfish manipulation by some special interest, or a search for market equilibria through which all may benefit from the more efficient allocation of resources? Would price controls benefit citizens in the short or long run? Is the air they breathe, or the water they drink, seriously damaging to their health? What would they have to sacrifice to effect an improvement? Are changes worth it? How should the civilian leadership control the military? Are threats to national security from a neighboring nation-state, described by leaders in ominous terms, genuine or simply a scaremongering mirage? Do such threats justify the sacrifice of resources that would be required for rearmament?

Without access to information and reasoned argument citizens are not able to take a meaningful part in liberal democracy. Without this access they are likely to stand in the way of policies that may be in the best interests of society, as well as their own. They may reject policies that they do not adequately understand out of frustration and suspicion that goes back to the authoritarian tradition from which they are just emerging. Social consensus rooted in the confidence that emerges from citizen understanding is as important to a stable democracy and an efficient economy as are the franchise, property rights, and free markets. The mentality of bitter confrontation and blind intervention that characterizes an authoritarian regime is never far from the surface in a society in transition to a democracy, and new habits of tolerance and understanding must be nurtured and carefully preserved.

For the long run, education that is both broad and deep must be the base upon which citizen understanding and informed participation rest in a democracy. The press and mass media are a crucial part of this educational system, especially for adults who have moved beyond formal schooling and must acquire information on their own initiative. In a society in transformation to democracy the media play an especially critical role because they serve not only those who would sustain their comprehension of policy issues but also those who for all or part of their lives have been excluded from open inquiry.

The functions of the press and mass media in a free society may be grouped under six headings.

(1) *Delivering the facts.* The mass media facilitate the flow of information between sender and receiver and reduce thereby the costs of ignorance to both parties. In well-behaved modern media facts are transmitted in two forms, one reflecting the needs and wishes of the sender—what we call advertising (or propaganda)—and the other reflecting the needs and desires of the receivers as perceived by the media—what we call conventional reporting. In all media everywhere there undoubtedly occurs some blurring of these functions. In authoritarian regimes typically the first overwhelms the second; in healthy democracies there is a clear demarcation and reasonable balance between the two.

(2) *Presenting opinions and analyses.* The news media may present opinions on facts and interpretations of events in four different ways: in news reports that include the opinions of persons outside the media; in news analysis by specialists on the staff; in editorials and columns; and in guest appearances by nonjournalists in what are often called in the United States "op- ed" pieces (opposite the editorial page), forums where varied expert opinions are aired. The most potentially controversial way to present opinion in countries where the press is tightly controlled or monitored is the third of these: editorials and columns. This requires the medium itself to take and defend a position, a process that calls for skill, tenacity, conviction, and, often, courage. A demonstrated commitment to what it publishes or airs may be the medium's most valuable service to readers and listeners.

One of the most difficult tasks to execute skillfully is news analysis. While some journalists (and many readers) may have difficulty differentiating between fact and opinion, they are apt to become totally confused over that in-between and vague thing called "analysis." Basically, analysis is the art of interpreting and highlighting the significance of an event without expressing the writer's opinion or judgment on the issue. In the best American papers, this is used effectively to supplement hard-news stories of transcendent events, and is clearly labeled on the printed page as "analysis." But it is *not* opinion, and its effective execution is a highly polished craft. As for the other methods, reporting the opinions of others is the centerpiece of standard news reporting, and requires no commitment or position by the reporter. Enlisting guest opinion makers also alleviates the paper's responsibility for what is said, and guest columns can be dropped, repudiated, or "balanced" at any time the political climate seems to demand it.

(3) *Conducting investigations.* Exploration of circumstances and the conduct of sophisticated inquiry into causes are as much the legitimate responsibility of mature media in a civil society as are the communication of simple facts and opinions. But these functions are also the most difficult to perform successfully. They require highly sophisticated and experienced staff, specialization in critical areas of inquiry, and relationships with scientific and scholarly communities that may take years to develop.

One particular variant of investigative reporting is penetration of political events in search of departures from the law or ethical norms. In this function the media conduct in effect a political post audit, a task assigned in political theory typically to the "loyal opposition" but in the modern age often performed by an external agent. Efforts by the press cannot, of course, ever be comprehensive or a fully satisfactory substitute for other monitoring agents, because of the cost and time required. But press investigations are important instances of independent oversight that signal needs and opportunities to other actors, often including universities, think tanks, interest groups, and civic associations. Investigative reporting of political performance has become associated above all with the accomplishments of Bob Woodward and Carl Bernstein in the Watergate scandal—to the extent that the suffix "-gate" is now frequently attached to journalistic political exposés throughout the world.

As important as the external political post audit conducted by the media may be for the modern democracy, its cost may be the distraction it poses from serious, time-consuming, and far less dramatic and glamorous explorations into economic, environmental, social, or security issues. Tracking the peccadillos of politicians may grab the headlines (and sometimes the prizes), but over the long run, explaining the implications of actions in more prosaic areas may be more significant to the nation.

(4) *Entertainment.* The press and mass media are unusual in that they combine, in single products, services that provide at the same time information valuable to recipients, education on how to interpret this information, and

simple entertainment. In some cases these products are "joint," meaning that the generation of one necessarily leads to production of another (as when documentary dramas both educate and entertain). But very often these products are alternatives in production, and the danger is that one—entertainment—may crowd out the others.

(5) *Control.* It is practically inevitable that a totalitarian regime will use the press and mass media to maintain its grip on its subjects. It may do this by telling lies, by repressing the truth, by constraining information flows of all kinds, and by manipulating messages for a variety of ends. When a transition to democracy occurs, use of the media for control is one of the practices that is typically reduced or eliminated. One of the challenges to those who live through such transitions is to recognize and press for elimination of such elements of control.

(6) *Policy analysis.* There is a growing trend in the U.S. media (for example, the *MacNeil/Lehrer Newshour*, the *Washington Post*, and the *New York Times*) to present analysis of policy alternatives without necessarily offering conclusions or citing preferred alternatives. What are the options for the health care system? Which military bases should be closed, and why? Should the North American Free Trade Agreement (NAFTA) be modified, ratified, or defeated? The analysis of such questions requires a sophisticated understanding of the costs and benefits of alternative policy options, fairly presented. The media in Latin America are just beginning to engage in such reportage to convey to their readers, viewers, and listeners the range of choice available to them.

Two other functions, of major importance in the Latin American context but also true for some U.S. and European media dynasties, are to make money for press owners and to promote the political interests (and sometimes careers) of the owners and their allies.

Challenges to the mass media in emerging democracies are not different in kind from those in mature democracies, although they may differ in degree. Questions that demand attention include the following. How can prevailing attitudes from the former authoritarian regime, of either slavish adherence or bitter confrontation, be converted to a constructive search for reasoned understanding and social consensus? How can the mass media acquire and sustain skills in complex areas of inquiry that are important to a nation in the late twentieth century: economics, environmental science, health, international relations, national security policy, and others? What can and should be the contributions of universities, think tanks, and government itself? How should the profession of journalism be organized and protected under the law? What are the special rights and responsibilities of journalists? How much of their time and effort should be devoted to investigative reporting? Do journalists in emerging democracies perhaps have a special function to perform as auditor and conscience of the state, a function that may be performed in due course by other social institutions such as the legislature, the courts, and nongovernmental agencies? What are the dangers, to journalists themselves and to society, of assuming this role even temporarily? Does the organization of the media need to be regulated or restrained, in emerging democracies, to limit the abuses of economic power that may occur in any concentrated market and to recognize the social and political losses, in addition to economic inefficiencies, that may follow from media monopoly? More broadly, what are the proper relationships that should evolve between government and media? How much control? How much protection and public subsidy? Need a government worry at all about the welfare of the media, and vice versa, or might their mutual concern perhaps lead more to abuse than to protection of the public interest? How are the fast-moving electronic media of radio and television changing the set of questions that must be asked about media policy? Clearly these are questions that may be posed in democracies at all stages of maturity. Opportunities abound for collaborative and comparative responses.

This study describes primarily for North American readers conditions in the press and mass media in Latin America as they relate to opportunities for constructive north-south interactions. It is motivated by the questions listed above but seeks to understand them rather than to answer them. The authors are authorities neither in the field of communications nor in Latin American studies. But they bring to the study a long-standing research interest in public policy related to the economy, international security, international education, and the process of democratic transformation. In 1992 and 1993 they visited four countries in Latin America: Argentina, Brazil, Chile, and Mexico. Rich conversations were held there with reporters, editors, and publishers, with broadcasters and owners; with government officials, business persons, scholars, and shrewd observers of the societies in which they live. Because of the limited time available, attention was directed mainly to the media in the major metropolitan centers and capital cities. The pages that follow are a synthesis and interpretation of what was discussed. Separate chapters provide brief road maps of the recent history and current conditions of the media in each of the four countries. A summary chapter then reviews issues that seem of particular significance across all four countries. Finally, programs now in place in the United States that provide training and assistance to the Latin American media are reviewed, and future opportunities discussed.

The intent of this monograph is both to provide an interpretive account of the state of the media in the emerging democracies of Latin America and to offer suggestions on how U.S.-based programs could strengthen their capabilities.

The Media in Argentina: Serving the State Pro Tem

The Argentine Media in Transition to Democracy

As much as any country included in this study, Argentina has a long tradition of strong and vigorous mass media. The Buenos Aires daily tabloid *Clarín* is often described as the largest Spanish-language newspaper in the world. Other major dailies are *La Nación*, *La Prensa* and *Crónica*. They all tend to address different strata of society. The first democratic president of Argentina, Domingo Fausto Sarmiento (1811-88), was himself at one point in his career a journalist, and other respected politicians and intellectuals have traditionally contributed to the media.

The Argentine people read a great deal and are avid consumers of television and radio programming. Changes in their preferences cause frequent rises and falls in the fortunes of particular media. All kinds of tastes, including the most sophisticated, receive attention. For example, at present the highbrow political analyst Mariano Grondona appears on prime-time television before a large elite audience that seems comparable to that for *Washington Week in Review* in the United States.

Yet the Argentine media have suffered much from a half-century of repressive authoritarian regimes. More than 100 journalists were among the "disappeared" during the most recent era of military rule, and a climate of fear was accepted during those years as part of the job. Today such fear is mainly absent, but some journalists, at least, still sense a level of hostility from government that reminds them of darker days and is deeply troubling.

9

As in Mexico and some other countries of the region, government has traditionally tried to control or constrain the media through various devices that range from the distribution of radio and television rights to payments for advertising, restrictive regulation of television and radio licenses, intimidating lawsuits against journalists, selective release of news and operation of newsprint cartels. Some optimists believe that the reduction in the size of the state now in progress through privatization, including the sale of state-owned media, will help to reduce the incentives for intervention and the number of levers by which government can influence the media. Pessimists are doubtful.

Virtually everyone who observes the Argentine press today concedes that this is a time of major adjustment and search for balance among competing values. Government has had to adapt reluctantly to the fact that the media in a democracy tend to serve more as critic than as lobbyist or cheerleader. The news the media publish and the spin they give it are entirely different in a democracy from what is permitted to be offered in a tyranny. The media, in turn, have had to gain self-confidence and a new assertiveness as they turn from government to consumers for their patronage. The consuming public for its part has called upon the media to absorb and comprehend monumental events—a war, a coup d'état and a transition to democracy—all in just 14 years.

The Challenges of Public Policy

Argentina is today witnessing a critical clash between two ideologies that have a virtually religious status among different groups within the country: Peronism, intended to be a middle way between communism and capitalism, and free-market neoliberalism that sees solution in a reduction in the power of the state. Yet neither has been explained carefully to the wider public or analyzed for relevance to critical issues of the day. These are tasks for which the media should be uniquely prepared. That the media have had neither the time nor energy to do this effectively is one of the prices of constraining authoritarianism.

Most observers conclude that the Argentine media are not well organized today to perform either the informational, critical-interpretive or policy-analytic functions allotted to them in democratic theory. If stable democracy is to be achieved, fundamental reform of the media will be necessary. To begin with, there is excessive concentration of market power. *Clarín*, with daily circulation of 600,000 and weekend circulation of about one million, is a formidable— even overwhelming—presence in the market. In addition, *Clarín*'s owner, the

Noble group of companies, is both a multimedia conglomerate, with the largest nationwide radio coverage by satellite as well as a major television channel, and a diversified conglomerate, with related activities including a newsprint company and a wire-service news agency. Though some discussion of concentration of media power has occurred in the Argentine Congress, there is no settled policy that addresses issues of vertical or horizontal monopoly, multimedia ownership, foreign control and other important questions related to communications.

Despite the size and vigor of many of the mass media in Argentina, most observers complain of the relatively low and demoralized state of the profession of journalism. During the years of repression journalism was not an attractive career option because of the constraints on action, and schools of journalism and communications did not train practitioners for the democratic social role that lay ahead. There are no effective press laws that protect journalistic sources or the right of journalists to speak out. The journalists' union professes some of these objectives, but it is relatively weak. One observer noted that the question often asked is "not whether a story is true or false, but why it is being published."

Continental European traditions influence the Argentine media at least as much as North American ones, and this confusion of models may be part of the problem. Argentina and Chile are the most "European" of Latin American nations in immigrant composition and cultural outlook. It was noted that *La Nación*, for example, reflects nineteenth-century French circumspect journalism. To the Argentinian upper classes, Britain and the European continent have always been the preferred model to the United States. Views negative toward the United States were reinforced during the Malvinas War, when Americans became known as the "people who betrayed us . . . who helped the British kill our kids." The Madrid daily *El País* is often named as the most influential role model, and the wide participation of intellectuals part-time in the media that is common in Europe is an important feature of the Argentine press. As the universities have crumbled under financial stringency and neglect, the desire of academics for new channels of social communication has grown, and they have turned more and more to the mass media. In many cases this has strengthened the media, but it may also have retarded the growth of a strong full-time journalistic profession. Moreover, it may help to explain the paucity of balanced, open-minded, "unpositioned" career journalists. There has not been any pressure for exclusionary restrictions against "amateur" uncredentialed journalists, as there has been in Brazil.

Cadres of well-trained and informed journalists with experience in special fields like economics or the environment seem not to exist in Argentina. The enterprising and imaginative generalist is the most familiar model. In the view of one observer, "persons with little academic training and few scholarly contacts predominate among the most successful reporters." Editors and publishers seem not to deplore this situation; indeed they strengthen it by providing little mid-career specialized training or sufficient time for journalists to pursue stories in depth.

One serious concern among many observers of the Argentine media today is that the corrupt practices of the general society have moved into the media as well. While journalists assiduously pursue corruption in government, they seldom report its presence in their own midst. One businessman spoke eloquently and angrily about the media corruption he encounters regularly. He claims that reporters repeatedly confront him with various forms of "shake-down" or blackmail. He is asked to engage certain reporters as consultants lest they carelessly print negative information about his firm. Other reporters offer—for a fee—to "check" stories about his firm with him before publication, so that he may "correct mistakes." He admits that such bribes and payoffs reflect a long-standing cultural heritage, but he is convinced that these practices cannot be consistent with the status of an efficient modern market economy and mature democracy to which the country aspires.

The alleged corrupt practices of the media about which this and other businessmen complain, and toward which they believe owners of the media are complacent (because as a result they may pay lower salaries), seem somehow more venal than the practices in Mexico of payments to journalists that are at least more thoroughly institutionalized and aboveboard than those induced by a shakedown. To the extent that these corrupt practices are as described (which is difficult to determine), the journalists involved seem more like petty criminals than professionals. They are insensitive to conflict of interest and unfaithful to the ethics of their craft.

The Political Role of a Vanguard Press

As in Brazil, journalists in Argentina have gained their greatest fame through investigative activism of the Woodward and Bernstein kind. This atmosphere, they say, is reflected in radio and on television, where interviewers have learned how to ask tough and embarrassing questions. Reporters recount that at press conferences in the days immediately after the return of elected government few questions were asked, because under the military regime questions from the floor had always been planted by the authorities. Ironically, from this reticence, self-censorship and enforced respect for authority, it has been only a short step to intense cynicism about and disrespect for government, to the point that some moderate observers now deplore the prevailing mood of confrontation between press and government on even minor matters. In the long run this may be counterproductive to both.

This regret is rooted in two concerns. The first is that democracy may be like a fragile blossom in Argentina, which will wither and fall under the kind of stress created by a vicious watchdog press. The second is that the press's overwhelming attraction to issues of personality, petty scandal and partisan political affairs has distracted it from attending to the enormous public policy questions that face the nation. Perhaps most illustrative of the legitimacy of this concern is the fact that the neoliberal reforms of President Carlos Menem have moved the country away from a Peronist, statist, cooperative emphasis on constrained markets and a large public sector with almost no serious public debate. Regardless of where one stands on the wisdom of the reform, this change above all others is one upon which Argentine citizens should surely be very well informed and upon which they should have their say. The process of reform has been complex and multidimensional, involving among other things the dismemberment of a substantial public sector. In addition to this systematic, virtually constitutional, change, issues of the environment and foreign policy also call out for balanced and sustained attention from the public and the policy-making elites. These questions have all been submerged, understandably but sadly, beneath continuing fears of a return to authoritarian rule and abuse of human rights, clashes of personalities and family scandals.

Some observers, however, remain cynical that Argentinians care that much about democracy. In their view, the skyrocketing inflation that plagued the Argentine economy for many years is the overwhelming concern of most citizens. Even the personal escapades of President Menem, which the people follow with amusement in the press, are tolerated because of his ability to control this economic disease. As one analysis of the scene concluded, "With low inflation, Menem could wed ten women and dance till dawn, and nobody would care" (*Time International Edition*, 13 July 1992, 17).

In the vanguard of Argentine journalism today is a feisty and combative newspaper, curiously entitled *Page Twelve* (*Página Doce*). It came to life in 1987, after military rule, during the first democratically elected government of President Raúl Alfonsín. At the time there were threats of a new coup d'état by the military, and to resist this possibility a local entrepreneur began the paper with modest goals (including the 12-page format), employing a small group of journalists generally sympathetic to the Alfonsín agenda. Enthusiastic public response to the paper led to a more substantial product than had been initially anticipated. It now has a weekday circulation of about 100,000, with more on the weekend.

Initially only the multinational companies would advertise in *Page Twelve*, but gradually local companies were won over. The professional staff of *Page Twelve* remains remarkably young; the senior editors are still in their twenties! The most prominent (and senior) staff member is the immensely energetic and irreverent political correspondent and investigative reporter Huratio Verbitsky. He sees as his primary mission the establishment of free speech in the media. He believes that the paper has touched the conscience of the nation and, through humor, disrespect for authority and irony has awakened the public to the need for unconstrained self-examination.

The main reason for the impressive local readership of *Page Twelve* seems to be the steady stream of scandals that it unearths in the military, the privatization process and the personal lives of colorful politicians. Those who have been exposed have accused *Page Twelve* of being, among other things, the tool of drug barons, journalistic criminals and the manifestation of a Jewish conspiracy to destroy the state. But the critics have not succeeded in imposing silence. When the authorities strike back, the paper's favorite weapon is simply to tease. On one occasion *Page Twelve* was vilified as "the Yellow Press" by the president himself; it responded by printing the next issue on yellow paper. *Page Twelve* is not a paper that brings all the news to its readers. Typically it is read in conjunction with a conventional daily like *Clarín*. Its stock in trade is candid and irreverent comment on public affairs. Some claim that Verbitsky and *Page Twelve* play the role in contemporary Argentina that Jacob Timmerman played during the darkest days of military repression: a conscience for the people.

The position many thoughtful observers in Argentina take today on the role of vanguard publications in the media such as *Page Twelve* is that they must, at least for a time, assume some of the responsibilities that would normally be shouldered by other institutions in a healthier democracy, like the opposition in the legislature, the courts, and various nongovernmental institutions. These other institutions are in various ways and for various reasons weak and ineffective in Argentina today. Part of the problem is the ingrained political culture, and part the residual legacy of terror from military rule. Concentration of power is great, and traditional checks and balances are few. Consequently the press must in effect act as auditor and whistleblower for the pubic sector, as guardian of the national conscience, and as protector of a range of human rights, especially the right of free speech. For a time then, the media, although part of the civil society, must in effect serve the state.

It seems clear from what they have endured that the Argentine people remain unalterably committed to democracy. More than most societies, they have witnessed directly the horrific costs of unconstrained authoritarian rule. Their inoculation against tyranny should last for decades. Nor are many of the present-day military anxious to resume rule. They have discovered and been intensely frustrated by the complexities and headaches of governing a modern state. They seem happy to turn the job over to those who think they can cope. However, Argentina has not had very much real democracy since 1930 and is only now coming to grips with what the term means. In this environment the media can be pardoned for some unease. As one of our contacts commented, citizens have yet to learn that democracy means more than the right to elect a new dictator every six years (the length of the presidential term). True democracy will only come, it is argued, when the powers of the president are appropriately constrained and the rights of citizens protected. And these are the objectives of the vanguard press.

Where the press alone seems effectively able to impose a measure of discipline on the executive, a country remains burdened with a political system that is badly in need of reform. In this condition the press's responsibility must be to ferret out the relevant facts and present them to the people without fear or favor. In the view of one shrewd political observer, the press and other news media in Argentina today are more important then either the Congress or the judiciary as an effective countervailing force on the executive branch. A member of the legislature confirmed this view: "If Congress or the courts today say 'scandal,'" he explained, "no one believes or pays attention to it; if a journalist says it, then they do. The press has a lot of power because it has in its favor the presumption of objectivity." At the same time he bemoaned the scant attention devoted to congressional affairs by the media and claimed that this inattention itself contributed to congressional irrelevancy. Most commentators agree that this responsibility of oversight overburdens the media. Yet there is no choice at the moment but that the press accept it, because the other relevant institutions have declined to take on the task.

One prominent editor claims quite simply that Argentina has become one of the most corrupt nations in the world, with bribes and payoffs almost universally affecting both the efficiency and the moral fiber of the nation. He finds this climate of corruption, present in the private sector, ubiquitous in government. The singleminded focus on this phenomenon by some of the more courageous sectors of the media is thus neither sensationalism nor an unwholesome prurient interest in scandal. It is, in his view, based on a legitimate judgment about political priorities. Political corruption has to be rooted out before conventional public policy issues can be addressed. Close monitoring of the executive is an exhausting and at times terrifying task for the press. The courts are one of the government's main weapons against the press, sustaining convictions for such infractions as "disrespect for authority"!

One of the reasons why various parts of the media are nevertheless assuming this oversight role with some alacrity, it is suggested, is from a deep sense of guilt. During the years of military rule, when some thirty thousand citizens disappeared, the media remained largely silent; they now believe they have much for which to atone. The hope is, of course, that as political institutions, especially the legislature and the courts, regain their balancing role against the executive, the press may be able to return to other more conventional tasks, including in-depth explorations of public policy options of various kinds. In due course the Argentine people must find and defend an appropriate relationship between the state and civil society. At the moment the state perceives civil society and the media mainly as a threat, not as an essential complement, and this leaves the media on the defensive much of the time.

The Media in Transition

Parts of the media in Argentina today feel like David facing a menacing Goliath, or the Dutch boy with not enough fingers to stop the holes in the democratic dike. They see themselves as guardians of the flame of liberty. Their cause is a noble one and they are recognized widely for it in other nations. They have from time to time received encouragement and assistance from abroad through groups like the Committee to Protect Journalists, the magazine *Index on Censorship*, and on one occasion even from a number of U. S. congressmen. But in many respects the greatest challenge lies ahead.

Unquestionably an important task of the media in a democracy is to challenge and expose those who would threaten and subvert freedom. This task at least some part of the Argentine media have assumed with courage and success. When that work is complete—or, rather, well in hand—the next task of the media is to help citizens engage in a conversation among themselves and with the state to explore policy options and reach consensus about those that are most acceptable and desirable.

In both these efforts the Argentine media may benefit a great deal from overseas contacts. They may benefit enormously from help in sorting out their analytical objectives, in testing their progress against the experience of journalists elsewhere, and through worldwide publicity to gain protection and strengthen their resolve. The Argentine media have accomplished much already, but there is so much more to do, and bountiful opportunities for those outside to help.

The Media in Brazil: Throw the Rascals Out

The Media in Political Life

Like almost all the countries of Latin America, Brazil has since World War II endured a period of military rule (1964-85), with some harsh repression but nothing as severe as that in Argentina or Chile. The consensus is that unlike their counterparts in Chile and Mexico, the Brazilian media emerged from repression with considerable credit. They resisted and worked around censorship, using all kinds of codes, double meanings and other stratagems. The Brazilian media overall are widely perceived to be the strongest in Latin America, economically secure in most cases, technically sophisticated and, with a few exceptions—most notably concerns that have encountered financial difficulties and accepted state assistance—independent of government. Comparing the Brazilian media with those in other Latin American nations, one prominent local journalist suggested that "Mexico is an unofficial joint venture between the media and government. In Brazil, by contrast, the written press at least has spent much of its time struggling for independence from government."

In the recent aftermath of authoritarian rule, some adjustment was required from media attitudes of self-censorship, but in general this has been accomplished. Yet although the present situation is nothing like as constrained as in Chile, some sacred cows still roam free. One television producer observed, for example, that "Only [the weekly magazine] *Veja* has the strength to take on the Bank of Brazil." Print media directed toward the elites naturally remain concentrated in the two major cities; even the most successful (e.g., *O Estado* and *Folha* in São Paulo) have a circulation of only a few hundred thousand. *Veja* by contrast enjoys a circulation of more than half a million. The magazine *Impresa* is concerned specifically with journalistic issues but is essentially by the media for the media.

Although formal censorship ended in the 1970s, democracy returned only gradually over the years 1974-85. During that interval the media were widely credited with legitimizing the opposition. Following a French tradition, intellectuals were expected to speak to and for the people at times of crisis, and many media opened space for that purpose: *Folha de São Paulo*, in the lead, reserved its "Page 3" for such commentators. In the long run, however, this wide use of outsiders during the repression may have weakened the media by reducing the need for well-trained, full-time, staff specialists in subject areas. There is, for example, still no resident media authority on the European Community—a subject highly important to Brazil—or on constitutional law, after nearly a decade of debate on that topic. It is striking that many journalists with important substantive expertise are now nearing retirement, whereas investigative reporters are mainly quite young.

Since the 1970s the media and other social institutions collectively, but not collaboratively, have been exploring their proper role vis-à-vis the polity and the economy. By and large other social institutions have been a major disappointment: little effective political leadership has emerged, and the economy has experienced relatively slow growth and exceptionally high inflation. Largely by default, the media have thus assumed toward both these entities the role of inquisitor, auditor and goad.

Some critics argue that in this role the media have gone too far. Yet their powerful working asset, according to one prominent journalist, has been the shame of the Brazilian people. Unlike the Mexican people, he argues, who have accepted the principles of limited democracy, Brazilians have retained high ideals and have responded to exposés of corruption and incompetence with indignation and fury. "That Collor crowd from Alagoas broke all the rules," he complained. "They stole so much money they broke down the façade of honesty, and that was unpardonable. Their blatant excesses threaten to ignite the flames of mass indignation and bring the whole system down." Another veteran journalist suggested that, much as the press anywhere is a mirror of society, the Brazilian press, like the people, still feels anger and betrayal for the period of repression: "The press is taking revenge for the years of suffering. It talks too much without a sense of responsibility. It scowls all the time because it hates the government." No one, he insists, should push for too much reform in the media. Time will bring modulation.

Moreover, "variety and diversity, both good and bad, ultimately lead to greater strength in the media just as in nature."

The defining moment for the nation, and for the press in particular, was the exposé, and then the departure in 1992, of the recently elected president Collor, in which the press took a critical part. After this heady and immensely exhilarating episode, however, the Brazilian media have had to return once again to more prosaic tasks and fundamental questions from which they were temporarily distracted. And they have had to reflect on what that signal episode portends for the long run. One permanent change brought about by the Collor incident, says a major owner in the media, is that "the myth of government as an omnipotent, impregnable stronghold accessible only at intervals by the vote has been exploded. All sorts of groups—business, labor and others—have discovered that they can challenge government success-fully through the media. As a result, a new sense of community has been created." This has given the Brazilian media, or some part of it at least, a sense of its own destiny that is absent in the other neighboring countries with similar background experience.

Distinctive features of the Brazilian nation are its tremendous size, large and varied population, rich culture and unquenchable zest for life. The complexity of Brazilian nationhood is unique among the countries we visited. One observer describes it as an elephant with no bones, another as a continent with five countries inside it, with a "first-world population" of only ten million or 15 million, and therefore a media market like that of Belgium or Holland, not the United States. It is estimated that only about one-third of the total population of some 150 million is truly literate (that is, with four years or more of grammar school), and a large proportion of the population lives far from major urban centers. This provides an exceptional opportunity to the elec-tronic media, and Brazilian television (especially the Globo network, with 75 percent of the market) is among the most advanced in the world.

The print media are confined to the literate one-third, and the elite press is concentrated heavily in the two major population centers of Rio de Janeiro and São Paulo. The large, big city dailies, television networks and glossy weekly newspapers are all very strong in Brazil. The venerable Rio daily *Jornal do Brasil* has faced financial crisis recently (perhaps because it has no links with television or radio), while the daily *Folha de São Paulo* has forged ahead to assume a national role that some compare to that of the *Washington Post* or *The New York Times* in the United States. The weekly news magazine *Veja* is the strongest of its kind in Latin America. The smaller journals of opinion and regional newspapers are much weaker. A growing problem with multimedia ownership seems to be that "package" contracts for advertising across media (for example, between the Globo newspaper chain and TV Globo) may drive individual independent media out of existence.

Some people marvel that with its size, complexity and innumerable inner tensions Brazil has survived as a nation at all. One commonly suggested explanation is the "clientelist" character of Brazilian social relationships. As in medieval feudalism, people are closely bound by reciprocal rights and responsibilities. One of our informants pertinently cited a popular Brazilian aphorism: "For my friends, everything. For those I do not know, nothing. For my enemies, the law." For the media a clientelist state presents many complexities.

Dynastic private control is predominant; it is no exaggeration to say that fewer than a dozen families control the large majority of the media. Even more significant than this concentration of market power are these families' clientelist relationships with many other sectors of society that are reflected in the media. In this they resemble the old Scottish clans in some respects, complicating all phases of social, political and economic life through powers and obligations passed vertically through generations and horizontally by marriage. Such proprietary relationships not only introduce bias into news reporting and interpretation but also nurture prevailing suspicions among readers who presume that there must always be much more to a text than meets the eye.

Typically these media owners have political views—but not political careers—that they wish to advance. They have worked out various understandings with their journalist employees (who are usually more radical politically), restraining them only when owner interests are directly affected. From time to time governments too have used a wide range of tactics to "influence" the media, including the distribution of advertising, contracts for printing such government documents as the phone directories and low-interest loans. Nevertheless the Brazilian media have succeeded in maintaining a higher degree of autonomy than, say, in Mexico, where similar devices are employed.

In general, media owners were disgusted with the corruption and mismanagement under President Collor and his regime, and once attacks on him had begun even the most dependent media were able to join in. Indeed to some observers the Collor episode devolved into an unhealthy "piling on" by owners and journalists who scented the blood of a mortally wounded animal and pursued a sensational scandal that would boost revenues. Certainly this convergence of interests was scarcely an occasion where journalists' independence from the owners could be tested. Nor were attacks on a crippled administration necessarily strong evidence of a free press. In the words of one critic, it was merely "an action of a libertine press."

Unlike the elites of the three other countries examined in this study, Brazilian leaders are reasonably content with their media. One former cabinet member and central bank president commented that the nation's educational system had failed, which thus placed a heavy responsibility on the media for the "formation of public opinion." This he thought they did quite well. He also thought the media's presentation and interpretation of the facts was quite adequate. He remained concerned primarily about their tendency to exaggerate and sensationalize. He was likewise uncertain whether the media could muster the power to overcome some of the crucial intellectual impediments to development. Every country, he says, has myths that are part of the culture. Some of these limit constructive action. In India the myths are religious; in Brazil they are economic, and make policies to combat inflation and stagnation difficult to introduce and to implement. Myths about the causes of income distribution are too deeply ingrained in the culture to be confronted by journalists alone. Other contributors to Brazilian intellectual life must sustain the media in this task.

It is difficult to gain a clear sense of the extent to which the present Brazilian government exercises repression or attempted control of the press. Such interference appears to be far less pervasive than the sophisticated system we saw in Mexico or the aggressive approach used in Argentina, but it cannot be likened to the general respect for social consensus that seems to prevail in Chile. Extensive conversations with reporters and editors yielded numerous accounts of threats against the media and of occasions when ministers and lesser officials have interceded forcibly to constrain the publication of damaging material. As several observers pointed out in regard to the image of total press freedom that emerged from the celebrated Collor case, it must be recalled that the media knew a great deal but said nothing out of fear until the prestigious *Folha de São Paulo* broke the silence and made it safe for others to speak.

Investigative Reporting: Triumph or Travesty?

Many commentators describe the Brazilian media as the saviors of the republic. After all, it was they, not the courts, the police, or the legislature, that exposed the scandal in the presidency. The magazine *Veja* and the newspaper *Folha de São Paulo* picked up the damaging testimony from the president's brother and pursued the story into all the dark corners that opened up. Other institutions of government and society only followed when they could no longer ignore the publicity. The challenge of bringing a president to his knees, admirers say, was met by a new, young generation of journalists, increasingly professional and distinct from the diploma-oriented restrictionist journalists who represented the old Brazil. This new generation, by one account, "shed light in a dark room while it was being burglarized."

But many others hold a less ecstatic view. On the timing of the Collor incident, they note that the scandal was virtually brought to the press on a silver platter. It had been percolating behind the scenes for months, unattended by the press. To make matters worse, they say, the press picked the morsel off the plate depressingly late, perhaps because media owners—at least before the presidential election—were concerned that Collor's opponent Lula, whom they liked even less, would be elected. According to one experienced television journalist, it was only after Collor had reached an unacceptable level of corruption that the Brazilian elite, represented in the media by the owners, "let the genie out of the bottle and let the press go after Collor full tilt!" The print media began the attack because they do not depend on renewable concessions from the government, unlike the electronic media. Television and radio were able to follow quickly by reporting not the facts but what the press had printed about the facts. No Brazilian Woodward and Bernstein rooted out the truth or cultivated a "deep throat" in the Watergate tradition. Indeed had there not been a Collor family feud, there might never have been an exposé. True, the media exhibited bravery in standing up to authority; yet by the time most of the media joined the chase the prey was fully on the run and posed no serious danger to them.

Moreover, critics claim, the press often violated principles of good journalism and individual rights. They published rumor, gossip and innuendo all mixed up with hard fact. Those accused of crimes were assumed to be guilty, rather than innocent until proven otherwise. In consequence, critics say, the media damaged reputations unfairly and confused entertainment value with serious news of a genuine betrayal of public trust. Close observers of investigative journalism in Brazil claim that it has seldom been based on hard fact and that the country can boast few well-briefed and hard-hitting investigative reporters of the Barbara Walters or Ted Koppel caliber. Investigative interviewers on television tend to treat with respect even the most venal guests on talk shows and seldom "drive them to the wall" in the manner of, say, an American Sam Donaldson or a British David Frost. Far too often reporters, including investigative reporters, become much too close to their subjects. There were occasions during the last presidential election when reporters greeted their favorite candidate at the start of press conferences by singing his campaign jingle.

What thoughtful observers seem to bring away from "Collorgate" is the appreciation that when the organs of the state fail the nation in preventing mischief, as they did in that instance, the media have an opportunity, and perhaps an obligation, to intercede. But when they do so they have a special responsibility to behave professionally and fairly toward everyone involved, remembering always that they are substitutes for organs that have developed practices over centuries that provide safeguards for all parties concerned.

For the long run, two conclusions may be drawn. First, training of the media for investigative reporting should be especially thorough and rigorous. Second, even under the best of conditions, vigorous watchdog media cannot be as satisfactory a means of safeguarding the integrity of the state as effective components of the executive, legislative and judicial branches of government designed for this purpose. It is necessary for those who assume the tasks of oversight to reject all unfair or unsubstantiated charges (no matter how newsworthy), to observe rules of evidence, to follow leads long after the drama of their discovery has receded and in all respects to remain analytically detached from public excitement. It is just as possible for a group of journalists to become a lynch mob as for anyone else.

The most cynical commentators on the Collor affair go so far as to suggest that in this case a journalistic lynch mob was assembled and let loose by an elite group of media owners who had concluded that the president had become inimical to their interests. By this interpretation the downfall of a president brought on by the media was less a triumph than a threat to stable democracy. If this could happen so easily to a bad leader, it might happen to a good one as well. The number of times that people mentioned one person—Gilbert Dimenstein of *Folha de São Paulo*—as the paragon of what a responsible Brazilian investigative reporter should be, suggests how rare this breed may be. Nonetheless the overall verdict on Brazilian coverage of the Collor affair was highly complimentary in the international press. As James Brooke of *The New York Times* noted, "In a landmark advance for Latin American democracy, Brazil's feisty press, independent Congress and professional police force dared to challenge and fully investigate the President's financial wizardry" (*The New York Times Magazine*, 8 November 1992, 33).

Correctly or not, many critics of investigative reportage in Brazil blame the popularity of this style of journalism on the dramatic impact of Watergate in the United States. One of the side effects of this focus on the office of the president, they say, is to misinform the public about the true nature of politics, and in particular about the important role of the Congress. During the repression, the military had begun making the Congress unworthy of press attention by reducing its powers. Collorgate has strengthened this sense of irrelevancy and sustained public inattention to the Congress after the return to democracy. "With all the drama of a soap opera given to it by the media," one critic argues, "Collorgate has contributed to the continuing depoliticization of the middle class."

Defenders of contemporary investigative journalism in Brazil respond to the charges of unfairness and limited real accomplishments, despite much publicity to the contrary, by countering that they have simply been overwhelmed by investigative challenges because other parts of society, notably the legislature, have been negligent and the press has not had the leisure to observe all the niceties. They also point out that truly effective investigative journalism requires a responsive public, whereas the Brazilian public has been so dulled and jaded by recent events that few things stimulate interest—the Collor scandal with its soap opera trappings being a rare exception. One reporter recounted his immense frustration when trying to rouse public protest against the rising tide of vigilante justice among the poor of the squatter camps around Rio and São Paulo. In one instance he produced a detailed account of the murder of nine people by a paramilitary group: reaction from readers was nothing at all. In such deafening silence it was difficult for even the most courageous editor to support him in more assignments of that kind.

The dust has not yet settled from the Collor affair. But when it does, clearly one important challenge for the Brazilian media will be to reach some judgment on the question of what role it should expect of investigative reporting in the future.

Topical Reporting in Depth: The Economy and the Environment

One of the principal functions of the media in a democracy is to inform members of the public about the facts and circumstances of policy areas that concern them. In addition the media have a heavy responsibility to provide citizens with the analytical equipment required to evaluate proposals for public policy alternatives that are presented to them by policymakers and others. Citizens need to understand the probable impact of these policies both on themselves and on some large conception of the public good. The media may fulfill these responsibilities directly, through efforts of specialists on their staffs or by transmitting analyses prepared by scholars, think tanks and other credible sources. Opinions differ over whether the Brazilian media are performing this function satisfactorily at the moment or are likely to do so in the foreseeable future.

One veteran journalist thinks that overall the conditions are simply too inhospitable to permit much constructive discussion and debate on policy issues in the media for some years to come. First of all, he explains, arguments over policy were dominated for several recent decades by Marxists and their critics. Now the demoralized Marxists have withdrawn from the field, but they remain hostile and mistrustful. The universities are in such crisis that their participation in policy debate has been affected very negatively. The most vocal journalists are also the most ideologically rigid and opinionated. The public who turn to the media for guidance on policy, he believes, can only come away confused. But it is possible to take a brighter view.

The policy area in which most Brazilians believe there is an urgent need for better understanding and national debate is the economy. After years of high growth in the 1970s, the 1980s and 1990s have seen stagnation, unacceptable levels of unemployment, much poverty and hyperinflation. Only the profoundly myopic can possibly argue that recent economic performance has been satisfactory. But what can be done to make it better? Various national economic models are much in vogue at the moment—Japan and South Korea are examples frequently cited by those who favor greater participation in a free world economy—and there is much talk of a Brazilian MITI (Ministry of International Trade and Industry) that would lead necessarily to social peace and prosperity. Free market ideology has gathered as many adherents in the past few years as dependency theory did at an earlier period, and perhaps without much more depth of understanding or recognition of the need for critical appraisal. No great national debate preceded the ideological shift, which probably is thus based on a shallow rational foundation. In particular, little attention has been paid to the complications introduced into a free market system by endemic public and private corruption, or the need to combat problems created by conspiracy in restraint of trade and unhealthy concentrations of market power.

A continuing puzzle is why the key issues for debate about the economy appear so seldom in the media—for example, the microeconomic question of efficiency in a free market system, and the macroeconomic question of how to deal with persistent inflation. The newspaper *Gazetta Mercantil* and one or two other publications cover market news effectively in the manner of *Barron's* weekly in the United States, but they provide mainly data and accounts of relevant happenings. They do little serious in-depth analysis or review of policy options.

One explanation of this mysterious silence is that readers and listeners lack sufficient understanding of even the most elementary economic concepts required for comprehension of sophisticated argument, let alone intelligent discussion and debate. Another is that inefficient markets and volatile prices have prevailed for so long that the populace cannot now conceive of anything else in the Brazilian context. One commentator referred to this condition as "social anesthesia." A third explanation is that, by and large, reporters and columnists themselves do not feel sufficiently comfortable with economic topics and concepts to discuss them in depth. The economics correspondent of one of the major daily papers lamented that he and most of his colleagues at other papers simply could not comprehend the economic conditions through which they were living and had no confident sense of realistic policy alternatives. He was particularly troubled that his editor and publisher did not seem to care. A fourth explanation for inattention to economic issues in the media is that influential elements in the elite benefit from the current economic conditions, or think they do. The last thing they want is public outcry that will lead to change. One economic reporter complained that he could not rouse any sense of outrage about hyperinflation in his publisher and editor, who seemed to find it an agreeable fact of life.

In any event, as one respondent put it, "No one is articulating the great economic issues for the public. The key economic issues seldom appear in the papers. Debate is conducted in private." He referred to the "Campari condition," whereby everyone in Brazil sits back, drinks a bitter cocktail of politics and lets the world go by. He added that some newspapers "have a tail sticking out that can be stepped on"—meaning that they are vulnerable to economic pressures because of their contracts with government agencies in other business activities (such as the printing of telephone directories). They are thus careful not to probe government policies too deeply or to pursue an analysis of economic policy too seriously.

The environment is another policy area where one might expect considerable action in Brazil. After all, this was the site of the "Rio Earth Summit" in 1992, and global advocacy against destruction of rain forests has been focused persistently and embarrassingly upon the Brazilian Amazon. Moreover, almost any visitor is bound to be struck by the contrast between the country's stark natural beauty and the extreme water pollution in Rio and air pollution in São Paulo. And indeed, mounting environmental concern is evident in some of the Brazilian media, especially in those two urban centers. In both cities the local university offers a course in environmental studies. Several papers publish special columns on the environment, and there are two television series devoted to the field, one at 8:00 A.M. on Saturdays. Yet it is estimated that in all of Brazil today there are still perhaps only ten serious environmental journalists. One young environmentalist—of the kind that appeared in many countries around the world in the 1980s—explained just how difficult it is to specialize in this field in the Brazilian media today. After eleven years of school he completed a four-year course to receive a diploma in journalism. Then he took another four-year first-level degree in marine science (the nearest thing he could find to environmental studies), concentrating on ocean pollution; he ended up the top student in his class. Upon completion of his education, he was employed by one of the major Rio dailies—and assigned to the city desk! In his opinion, the leaders of the Brazilian media do not know enough about environmental problems to perceive what they do not know.

Moreover, he says, much of the environmental movement as it is conceived today adopts a first-world style, but only a small proportion of the Brazilian population has first-world incomes and therefore first-world sympathies. He further claims that desertification in the Brazilian Northeast, caused by poor land management, is as serious a problem as destruction of the rain forest but has received almost no attention in the media. He pointedly complains that most media representatives who are assigned to environmental issues spend their time translating telexes from abroad, when they should be forging links with local scientists.

One major problem with all "science reporting," another journalist told us, is the short attention span of the reading and listening public, a phenomenon not unique to Brazil. Hot topics of the moment might be the dangers in nuclear power and offshore drilling. But no sooner has one begun to master those than public concern is likely to shift to the effects of alcohol combustion on the atmosphere or some other subject. An older journalist spoke with deep emotion about the problems he had faced over a lifetime of trying to raise public interest in environmental concerns. He commented bitterly that the Brazilian public "cared more about the color of Prince's underpants, Madonna's lovers, or the prospect of sending some minister to jail than the fate of the Amazon rubber tappers." As a reporter, he said, he tried to present the facts. But to "win the hearts and minds of his audience" he had to "create a reality based on emotion and sensation."

Although the government does not censor any science reporting, economic constraints remain in play. Any discernible diminution in its always very sparse audience, as a result of unappealing reportage, will prompt the cancellation of further coverage. Surprisingly, the Amazon area (the northwest third of Brazil) gets especially poor press. Not even *Globo* has an office there, and one of its reporters says the region is treated like a foreign country. Ironically, he explains, the growing consensus about the need for "sustainable development" in the Northwest has reduced controversy on the subject—and hence the attractiveness of related environmental reporting. "There are no environmental enemies any more, at least vocal ones," he says. This has reduced the opportunity to portray conflict: "Even God needs the devil."

The environment is, however, one policy area where journalists and scientists in universities and government are beginning to interact profitably, despite initial suspicion on all sides. There is a special need for this interaction, because available nonscholarly information is extremely unreliable. In the view of one well-informed observer, "The environmental movement is still mostly ideological and lacking in science." An added challenge is that the environmental movement is very diffuse, reflecting different regional and local circumstances. Thus it is no easy matter to cover environmental issues in Brazil, simply because of their scope.

One indication of increasing effectiveness in environmental reporting may be that the authorities are beginning to perceive it as a serious threat. The attention of some environmentalists, for example, is turning to destruction of the coastal Atlantic forests, which have even more biodiversity than the Amazon—and in which many powerful special interests have deep involvement. This is stirring up a real debate.

What environmental journalists say they need most is the capacity to evaluate complex policy options. "We can say what is right and wrong, but we cannot show the way ahead," says one leader in the field. "We are environmental marketers. We must learn to think globally and act locally. We need sustainable journalism."

Perhaps more than in all the other three countries we visited, some media professionals in Brazil showed a serious concern for deepening their understanding of special policy fields. The *Folha de São Paulo* in particular has moved in this direction and has held special forums to enlighten its staff and fill its pages on well-defined topics. Its "Page 3" is still celebrated as the citadel of pluralism.

A highly placed government official concerned with science and technology, and a distinguished engineer himself, is particularly critical of the state of science reporting. He thinks there are perhaps only two qualified science reporters in the nation. For this he partly blames the diploma system, which places a premium on "broad, thin knowledge." Television is especially weak. His government department is contemplating short courses for science journalists to help them ask good questions and write precisely. Now, he complains, they typically exaggerate and tend to side automatically with critics of authority, no matter how unsound they may be. Politics, he says, very quickly become hopelessly mixed up with science. A naive reporter can easily be manipulated by special interests in the science establishment who are seeking funding for some program or institute.

Electronic Journalism: New Frontiers of Communication and Democracy

Probably the most fascinating component of the mass media in Brazil today is television, in particular the Globo network, which has something approaching three-quarters of the market. During the years of authoritarian rule Globo accepted a role as virtually the propaganda arm of the military, whose leaders evidently realized that this was the route by which they must reach the mass of the people, upon whose acquiescence they depended to a degree. Globo has since developed a viewing audience of perhaps 50 million, including many of the nation's estimated 30 million illiterates, substantially on the basis of its productions of what are in effect soap operas (called *novellas*). The network broadcasts up to seven *novellas* per night, five nights per week. Technically very sophisticated (they are, incidentally, sold for distribution worldwide), these productions not only entertain but convey information and values of various kinds. They afford many examples of life imitating art. *Novellas* establish fashions: if a popular program deals with the 1960s, for example, fashions turn immediately to echo that decade. They also serve as a vehicle of instruction. When the government wished to stimulate an important immunization program, Globo portrayed popular *novella* characters receiving their shots and the populace followed suit.

The *novellas* sometimes also provide stimulus and context for discussion of critical social issues. For example, in one *novella* a domestic servant agonizes over whether to steal a school examination from her employer (a teacher) so that her son may gain a better life. In a country where poverty and crime are widespread and urgent policy issues, this dramatic portrayal affords an occasion for national reflection on the relationship between the two.

Critics of *novellas* complain that they encourage the ascendancy of a homogenized, consumerist society in Brazil, with a corresponding loss of distinctive national character. Others interpret this same process as constructive, aiding the modernization of a society that is largely illiterate and widely dispersed. Some would venture to claim that *novellas* have demonstrated the foolishness of uniquely Brazilian hierarchical and patriarchal relationships that retard development; after all, they have criticized even the military. Yet because Globo is so large and powerful, it must be cautious and moderate: there is no evidence that it has a well-formulated political agenda. *Novellas* are both liberal and conservative. If television were highly competitive and thus less "responsible," it could increase social volatility to the breaking point. And in the long run, some people speculate, television may be the only force strong enough to constrain the military.

Brazilian television has obtained a high level of technical accomplishment in other programming as well. News presentations and talk shows are very polished and professional. Indeed audience research discovered that many Brazilians believe the television anchors are hired from the United States because their style is so restrained and un-Brazilian. The network's large resources also benefit its international coverage. For example, three correspondents were sent to cover the Persian Gulf War in 1991.

Recognition of the political significance of television is embodied in legislation that guarantees each political party a modicum of free airtime before every election. (Collor's election victory is attributed in part to his skill in putting together a coalition of many small parties, each with its own free television exposure.) Television in general, and Globo in particular, has been closely aligned with the ruling elites in Brazil from the start. It was a measure of President Collor's abandonment by the elites that Globo fell in rather quickly behind the print media and exposed the scandal with all details to its legions of viewers. Because of the arbitrary way in which television licenses are distributed and renewed, it is necessary for Globo to maintain good relations with government over the long run. The attack on Collor was clearly mounted in anticipation of his imminent departure.

The powerful owner of TV Globo, Roberto Marinho, also operates a newspaper chain, which raises the difficult question of the propriety and social desirability of multimedia concentration. One of the reforms proposed by critics of the media in Brazil calls for distribution of television licenses in an objective process supervised by Congress instead of by the executive, and with a proportion reserved for nongovernmental organizations and other components of civil society. The entire field of public-interest television, which seems largely unexplored in Brazil, is beginning to attract some attention.[2]

One of the most distinctive features of Brazilian television, and to a degree all other media, has been the extent to which "external" forces have determined its content, especially of news reporting. During the years of authoritarian rule, first government and then the military called the shots. Now it is the owners (with a wary eye toward the government), their creditors and the sponsors. One news editor tells of a network owner actually standing at his shoulder while he prepared the evening news, to make sure the balance among the items met with his approval. A news producer said that no network is yet prepared to broadcast a story directly inimical to the interests of a major advertiser: "You are always getting phone calls saying 'please don't broadcast this or that,' and you don't." The newest external force affecting both television and radio is the church; not only the Roman Catholic Church but other denominations, like the Pentecostals, have been purchasing stations.

Among the most deplorable episodes in recent Brazilian media history was the lost opportunity, soon after the fall of the military regime, to introduce some reasoned method of allocating both television and radio franchises. Between 1979 and 1985 the last military ruler, General João Figueiredo, had granted licenses to 634 radio and television stations. Over the next three years the first democratically elected president, José Sarney, authorized another 1,028, thereby using up virtually all of the available channels and frequencies. We were told that throughout the decade the main criterion for the allocation of this scarce public resource was political expediency.

Restructuring of television and radio is high on the agenda of many political reformers in Brazil. They say that further democratization is impossible without greater pluralism of electronic communication. Informed popular choice cannot be achieved if information is channeled mainly through a single television network (Globo, with 70 percent of the audience nationwide from 6:00 P.M. to midnight) in a predictable, controlled pattern—many programs are taped, to prevent unwelcome spontaneity—and through radio stations that share adherence to the views of the president in power. Civil society, it is argued, cannot survive such concentration. In effect, by lack of access to varied media, people are being deprived of the freedom to form their own opinions. Opinions are formed for them. As if to complement—or complicate—the political role played by TV Globo, perhaps nearly 25 percent of radio stations are owned by elected political officials who also offer a constrained approach to the news.

Reformist think tanks and reformist social groups report that they can see their products on some subjects (such as the AIDS epidemic, though not land reform or the Catholic Church) into print and onto radio quite easily, but almost never into television. Part of their difficulty in penetrating the electronic media, they say, stems from their own unfamiliarity with the requirements, but no one is available to guide them toward adequate preparation. They claim that although technological advances have brought democratization of the electronic media within reach, it still eludes their grasp. Today one can start a radio station with as little as $1 million, but as outsiders they lack both the necessary licenses and even that modest capitalization. They advocate diversification and decentralization of ownership to include universities, local governments and nongovernmental organizations.

There is some faith that passage and implementation of broad antimonopoly legislation, such as that of the United States, with regulation and divestiture as remedies, would deal effectively with the antidemocratic consequences of a monopolized electronic media. Most critics felt a sense of pride in the technological sophistication of Brazilian television but regretted the political side effects of the present concentration of ownership and direction. Some charged that the owners of television and the richest segment of the elite are conspiring to sedate the mass of the people. "It is no coincidence," said one, "that we have one of the best TV systems in the world and one of most skewed distributions of income."

The Profession of Journalism

More than any other country covered in this examination, Brazil has treated very seriously the question whether journalism is a true profession, with all the rights and duties that appertain thereto, or is merely an employment category. If the former, as some believe, then the profession has certain standards to observe as well as various privileges and responsibilities that go with an assigned place in society. Four issues arise in particular concerning professionalization: first, whether it is socially desirable to require professional accreditation; second, whether journalists, because of their position as the "fourth estate," have a particular set of rights; third, whether they also have obligations growing out of their place in the social and political process, (and if so, what are these); and fourth, whether such rights and responsibilities should be embodied and protected somehow in statutes or the constitution, raising the activities of journalism thereby above the simple market relationship citizens have with the media.

As with all discussions of professionalization, the question of professional journalism may become entangled easily in controversy over just who is being protected by codes of conduct, diploma certifications, requirements for employment security and other limitations on the labor market. Typically professionals defend their claim to special status as protection of the public. In the case of journalists the public consists of consumers of the media who presumably may be exploited if not protected from unscrupulous and incompetent journalistic charlatans. Readers and listeners, it is claimed, may be seriously misled by purveyors of news and opinion who, like untrained doctors or lawyers, can impose suffering on a necessarily ignorant public.

Protection of the public is provided for in Brazil by a requirement that all journalists complete a diploma course at an accredited college of journalism or communications. While some working journalists find this a helpful constraint on the labor supply, few consumers who were consulted find this a worthwhile infringement on the market from their standpoint. Indeed some find it to be just the opposite. They argue that incompetent inside "professionals" are protected from the competence of talented outsiders, especially those who are unwilling to endure the drudgery of what is often described as dreary trade-school training for the diploma.

Some observers of Brazilian higher education claim that, ironically, the diploma requirement has actually contributed to the degradation of education for journalists. The guarantee of a market for their services has led faculties in journalism schools to delay necessary curricular reform. The most they have done is adopt the sonorous term "communications." One media owner complained bitterly that "the diploma excludes talented, creative and gifted people from employment in journalism, so they go into advertising, which has prospered. The worst journalists join the faculties of journalism schools, where they can't even teach their students how to write a story. With the diploma requirement, not even Pele would be permitted to become a soccer columnist." An editor lamented, "It is hard to find a really excellent young journalist today. There is no incentive for young people to go into the profession. The best young people go into law, business and advertising."

The present diploma certification requirement for journalism is consistently condemned by senior actors in the media—editors, publishers and owners alike. They say that this is merely an obsolete trade-union featherbedding device which benefits only the journalists themselves, especially the incompetent ones. To their mind the attributed public benefits are a mirage. They complain in particular that the certification requirements prevent them from invigorating the media by hiring staff who have exceptional, specialized competence in economics, law, environmental science, constitutional law or other fields. Such people, who should be crucial contributors to effective media in the 1990s, are simply unwilling to return to journalism school after reaching a high level of accomplishment in a particular field. Nor are many graduates of the relatively low-prestige journalism courses competent to return for specialized field training at a later date. And many of the most talented young journalists who have obtained the necessary certification bemoan the requirement and the waste of time in obtaining it as much as do the management. These circumstances are reminiscent of the situation in primary and secondary education in many nations, where talented individuals are excluded from the teaching profession by similar protective devices for those already in. Almost every editor and publisher who denounced the certification requirement for journalists explained to us various subterfuges they must and do employ to circumvent it. Some flout the system openly, inviting prosecution for admitted infractions.

The certification requirement likewise helps to explain the relative paucity of recognized and respected senior in-house columnists and pundits, and the prevalence of prominent academic and former government figures (such as Roberto Compos) as guest contributors. The distinguished columnist Castello Branco is described as perhaps the only remaining "heroic" Brazilian journalist.

As for the second major issue of professionalization—whether journalists have distinct rights that must be designated and protected against those who would infringe on them—among such rights are uninterrupted access to information (especially public information), confidentiality of sources and protection from all who would restrict publication of "the truth," be they the military, the church, advertisers or employers in the media or other interested parties. This last protection was described by one journalist as "the right not to reach a consensus."

On the third issue, whether the profession of journalism has distinct responsibilities as well as rights, feelings run as deep. The real question is whether journalists have a social obligation to think through the implications of their actions and perhaps pull their punches as a result. If a story truthfully reported will probably cause a riot, should the journalist report or print it? If democracy is fragile, does the journalist take actions that may endanger what liberty prevails, for example, by antagonizing the military? Should journalists expose conditions that will pit class against class, perhaps race against race or religion against religion?

Some would reply, absolutely yes! How can there be reform without hard-hitting inquiry? Who is the journalist to decide what the public should know? How can the journalist possibly discern consequences of actions when the best social scientists cannot? As one journalist put it, "There is no way to predict the positives and negatives of letting the monkey out of the cage." Another claimed that the notion of asking for restraint in reporting the news is like soliciting complicity in the exploitation of an ignorant, docile people. Still another suggested that this doctrine of the responsibility to exercise restraint in reportage had roots all the way back to the days of slavery, when limited information was one element in the control of the workers. Indeed, this respondent claimed, Brazil will not experience true democracy until it has a press that is at one and the same time well-informed, truly irreverent and freewheeling without a care.

On the other side, critics argue with great feeling that freedom can quickly become license. It is easy for observers in a mature democracy to say that consequences of excess can be ignored, but an emerging democracy cannot afford this luxury. One former government official put the case rather vividly: "There is no better story than Rome burning. Realization of this can turn a journalist into a pyromaniac."

The final issue related to professionalism asks whether the rights and responsibilities of journalists should be legally codified to reflect their unique importance to the health of the society and polity. One proposal currently afoot is for a law governing "democratic information" that would provide generally for free speech, freedom of information, municipal and regional radio and television broadcasting, public-interest programming, protection from political persecution, presentation of all sides of issues, encouragement of domestic film and video production and the appointment of a communications ombudsman. Evidently this was inspired by the examination of legislation in other nations, in particular the United States, France, Spain, Italy and Portugal, conducted in connection with the most recent revision of the Brazilian constitution. The media themselves have refused to give coverage to the proposal, and advocates are engaged in a word-of-mouth campaign to collect five million signatures to present to Congress. Even the authors of the plan doubt the possibility of passage under the present Congress, noting that nearly one-third of congressional members have financial interests in radio and television.

Criticisms of the idea of communications law take two directions. One suggests that regulation of any kind is likely to create as many problems as it solves, including some that are unanticipated at the start. The other says that the only genuine and long-lasting improvement in the media will come from cultural and social change that makes civil society appreciated and respected. Passage of a new law promises a quick fix that is not there.

Reflection on the desirability of communications law, no matter which way it turns out, does lead inevitably to consideration of many of the issues of communications policy that should demand the attention of leaders in any emerging democracy. One seasoned observer stressed that "media will change when society changes, not the other way around." But our own sense is that the process in fact is highly interactive, and that strengthening the Brazilian media would in itself yield important salutary effects on the society as a whole.

The Media in Chile: Finding a Delicate Balance

Conversion from Dictatorship

Authoritarian rule in Chile ended not with a bang but a whimper. President Pinochet was not driven from office; he withdrew when citizens, to his surprise, declined to approve an extended term as president. He has continued to serve as commander-in-chief of the armed forces, and many of those who had served with him in the military remain as well. This is a transition democracy in which the old regime was not fully dismantled. There is no *tabula rasa* for reform. Powerful interests from the authoritarian period, as well as elements of political culture, some institutions and rules of interaction, have persisted into the new democratic era.

The Chilean mass media cannot in most cases boast of a distinguished record during the years of military rule. Some are charged with having played a significant role in preparing the ground for the fall of President Allende in 1973. Later, under the heavy hand of Pinochet, they did little to protest human rights abuses. They were reportedly at least as compliant as the media in authoritarian Argentina, although in Chile governmental controls were exercised less through direct measures than through distribution of advertising, the price of paper, tariffs on printing equipment and other devices. Press conferences during the military period were fully regime-orchestrated, and journalists who asked the wrong questions lost their access and contacts. Government routinely provided "orientation" and "instruction" to the media. Pinochet's position seemed to be that the media had no right to know anything but did have the responsibility to report only what was pointed out to them—

often called "press-release journalism." Indeed the international press is generally credited with doing more to alert the Chilean people and the world to local human rights abuses than did the local media, with the important exception of certain news magazines. The Catholic Church, on the other hand, had a far more honorable record than the media and is remembered as one of the few effective centers of opposition, along with the independent "think tanks".

The consequence of this history and current condition is that the Chilean media are today still rather colorless and effete, certainly in contrast to those in Brazil and Argentina and in some degree to those in Mexico as well. The social-democratic government now in power has given up direct controls on the media and depends on "argument" and the "power to persuade." However, it complains that even with economic dependence gone, considerable psychological dependence on the old regime persists. The current political situation remains delicate; in the ever-present possibility of a new military coup, few seem willing to rock the boat seriously. The Catholic Church, strengthened by its courageous stand under repression (and its links to the current ruling party), has since grown more conservative and embarked on a crusade against the "moral crisis" that allegedly afflicts the country, including the media. Abortion, divorce and licentious behavior of all kinds are both proscribed by the Church and prohibited from public discourse. Formal censorship of the media, never very important in the Chilean case, ended with the return of civilian rule. But self-censorship operates almost as effectively.

Observers of the contemporary Chilean scene describe it in various ways. One spoke of "a conservative consensual society afraid of change in reality or image, with a popular government and a mild opposition." Another said, "Everyone is jumping to the middle of the seesaw." Still another described the press as merely a reflection of the larger society around it, wherein "no one will allow big thinking. Everyone fears losing the gains to date." Chile is committed to free markets and a free society, but few are presently willing to press for vigorous, unconstrained media or for reductions in concentrations of economic power, which in the long run are essential to such objectives. One senior government official stated simply that "no one talks about press reform because that implies a statist position, and that is out of fashion today." Another explained that "Chile is trying to emerge slowly and cautiously out of dictatorship with no fanfare. Government has settled upon compromise rather than confrontation as the best route to democracy and is uneasy about debate of the kind that a strong free press may generate. In general the population is divided between those who want to examine and debate the past and learn from it, and those who want to forget the past and start again with a clear slate and no bad conscience." Yet another commentator said, "The nation has two souls: one says make political compromise, the other cries 'justice.' "

The Mass Media Today

El Mercurio is the dominant daily newspaper in Santiago. Aligned loosely with the Pinochet government during the authoritarian period, it remains visibly skeptical of—although not hostile to—the post-Pinochet civilian government of President Patricio Alwyn. It is a modern, well-equipped paper but circumscribed in its news coverage and without major investigative or analytical accomplishment and ambition. The editor of *El Mercurio*, who makes a very reasonable case for the policy of his paper, observes that the Pinochet government fell leaving many highly controversial questions unanswered, including whether prominent national objectives should include revenge and reparations—a socially explosive condition. The working class in particular, he believes, feels shortchanged and betrayed and claims an "accumulation of social debt." With such large, potentially disruptive issues lying just beneath the surface, the media, including *El Mercurio*, have felt a responsibility to handle very delicately all such divisive questions as abortion, divorce, homosexuality and the extradition of the former East German leader Eric Hoenecker.

Many metaphors are used to explain contemporary dilemmas. When the woods are tinder dry, you start a campfire only with great care. New small wounds may simply open up other deeper ones and destroy the fragile political stability that now exists. The deeper wounds must be allowed to heal before the society enters into strenuous debate. Yet all indications are that these wounds are healing rather nicely.

The media, this interpretation suggests, reflect at the moment the social consensus of abhorrence of all controversy that might lead to upheavals and a return of repression. As one respondent put it, "The military left with their heads high, and they can always pivot on their heels and return." The possibility that such a return might occur, which was very real in 1990 when a second coup d'état seemed imminent, helps to explain the social-democratic strategy of nonconfrontation. The crisis in civil-military relations has been placed on the back burner. Working journalists practice restraint in reporting such issues, without any editorial instruction. Their attitude is reinforced by advertisers, who share in the social consensus on the need for tolerance and a spirit of reconciliation. *El Mercurio*'s editor predicts a revival of controversy first on topics where emotions remain relatively dampened—for example, the environment. He regrets the absence of skilled professional journalistic competence on such topics.

Not everyone is happy, however, with this truce-like condition. One critical observer of the daily papers complains that they are not contributing to the essential social growth of the nation: "They don't present policy alternatives, deep facts or the results of research. Their political analysis consists of reading a press release, contacting people with divergent views and allowing them to talk. Then they comment on the confrontation." Reporters, he added, are usually university graduates but poorly trained as journalists, lacking broadening life experiences. They can make little sense of developments in the economy, polity or international affairs. Virtually no authoritative columnists have appeared on the scene. Another critic expressed a cynical boredom with the media: "There is no snap, crackle and pop. At the moment there is not much investigative journalism because there is not much to investigate. It will be some years yet before anyone will burn the flag."

Ironically, considering the repression of the media under his regime, Pinochet vastly increased the number of schools of communications, to 30. But as in much of the rest of Latin America, most of the graduates go into advertising and public relations. One editor spoke angrily of the poor quality of the graduates he receives: "They have no foundation in a discipline. They can't think or write." A widespread lament from most commentators on journalism in Chile today is that the country sustains no center of high-quality teaching and research on the media and how they should evolve in the particular conditions that face the nation, taking into account the experience and conditions of the region and the world.

A research project already under way at a private think tank (the Center for Public Studies in Santiago, conducted by Miguel Gonzalez) aims to direct reflections on the media forward and away from the agonies of the past. Gonzalez reports that polls show that, perhaps because of the commitment to nonconfrontation, the media have not yet focused on the issues about which their readers care the most: health, law and order and local government. He is exploring the case for a new press law that will provide guarantees of journalistic access to information, press freedom and protection of the confidentiality of sources.

A rival paper to *El Mercurio, La Época*, was established in 1987 by Pinochet's opponents to help fight the "Campaign for No" that led to the president's retirement. It seemed quite natural during that era of sharp political division to have an ideologically divided press as well. *La Época* served its function well for several years, representing social-democratic ideas of reform against the conservative doctrine of the Pinochet regime's defenders. It was, we were told, "the voice for those who had no voice." Ironically, after Pinochet's departure, *El Mercurio* was able to adapt quite well to the new environment by moving closer to the center. *La Época* on the other hand apparently has not been able to move successfully from confrontation into an era in which its supporters are in office. It now faces financial crisis. In particular it has not managed to build the large circulation needed to attract substantial advertising revenues. As the editor describes the evolution, "Under Pinochet it was much better and more fun. We were a tribune for those who had no voice. Now it is quite boring as we attempt to become part of the analytical press." *La Época* may have to join a large publishing group and thereby lose its distinct identity. During the early years, the editor admits, the most important quality required of the paper's journalists was valor; "now it is competence, and that implies a different team." It had been hoped that *La Época* would have the same success as *El Pais* in Madrid, which grew with the strength of Spanish democracy. But in Chile the rival press was just too strong. One reported consequence of *La Época*'s current weakness is that President Alwyn's Social Democratic party feels somewhat misrepresented by the daily press, which, some government officials fear, may be attempting to interrupt or delay the transition to democracy.

Policy Issues for Attention

One critical public policy issue, raised especially by the operators of smaller media in Chile though (for obvious reasons) not heard in the three larger countries we visited, is whether economies of scale are such as to lead necessarily to a monopoly of the daily press. With *El Mercurio* deeply ensconced not only in Santiago but also in regional centers as well, is it possible for viable competitors ever to arise? Such a natural monopoly as *El Mercurio* seems to have may generate sufficient attendant social and political costs to justify some form of public subsidy to smaller competitors. At the moment the government's position is that the free market should prevail throughout the media. Thus pluralism may have to be achieved by representation of diverse views within a single strong medium rather than among competitors. One current exception to the official principle of laissez faire in the media is a government-sanctioned program, financed by the Inter-American Development Bank with European funds, to subsidize regional newspapers that increase coverage of local news. But overall the question of state intervention in the media market in order to increase competition has thus far not attracted wide public attention.

La Época's experience is a classic example of another obstacle to policy geared toward a competitive free press: media ventures that arise during times of struggle but cannot then survive an extended transition to democracy and certainly not a period of stability.

Nor has Chile enjoyed a rich tradition of weekly news magazines, perhaps because of the small market size that makes such publications uneconomical. One interesting exception is the magazine Qué Pasa. Founded in 1971 by a conservative businessman to confront the Allende government, it became at first a tribune for the right. During the Pinochet years it had privileged access to information, made an effective case for economic transformation to free markets and maintained an independent position on human rights. With a small circulation (about 20,000), the only way that Qué Pasa could survive during the 1980s was by including free books with its subscriptions; eventually in 1990 it went bankrupt. The magazine has since been revived, with a new commitment to a plurality of views and the goal of appealing to a wider and younger audience. It is the first Chilean news magazine to feature a strong economic section and to have established international exchange agreements for foreign news coverage with publications like Veja in Brazil and USA Today. Qué Pasa employs 19 young and energetic journalists but still has a small print run of only 30,000 (one-half are subscriptions). It plans to launch an investigative section modeled on that of Der Spiegel. How this magazine fares in the years ahead will indicate a good deal about the course of Chilean journalism. It may also help to suggest how other small nations can sustain weekly magazines of news and opinion and break from total dependence on similar magazines from larger nations. If Qué Pasa fails, Chileans—like citizens in many of the world's less populous countries—may have to face the choice between public support for such media or having none at all.

Practitioners of the broadcast media in Chile have stories to tell very much like those of the print journalists. But they view their record under military rule with greater pride. For some in radio and television, the years under the military were a peculiarly exciting time as these media pressed against the limits of repression, being repeatedly closed and then reopened and receiving some protection through intervention by the foreign press. The years of transition have in many respects proven more challenging. Broadcasters feel caught between the government's pronouncements about the need for public-interest programming, the tastes of their audiences and the prejudices of their advertisers. They have been particularly disappointed by the low ratings accorded to investigative reports, such as a public health item on the dangers of sausages. Evidently listeners and viewers are sated with horrors from the recent past and do not want to be informed or reminded of any more.

One television producer pointed out that when the nation does not want to talk about a subject, there is simply no way she can cover it effectively. The moral conservatism of the contemporary Catholic Church is also a constraint; when she aired a special inquiry into topless dancing, her viewers were outraged. Another program, a retrospective on the sociopolitics of torture, got very low ratings. People today want to hear only about the economy and the environment, she says. This is very frustrating because she feels a responsibility to lead them also toward other subjects in which they ought to have an interest. Her problems are accentuated by the youth of her staff, who have little experience with a broad range of subjects. The "lost generation" in Chilean journalism over the preceding two decades—those now in their thirties and forties—contribute by their absence or obscurity to the poor quality of both the print and broadcast media today.

One radio journalist still remembers with pride that his medium, more than television and print, explored and perfected ways to outwit the repression imposed upon it under Pinochet. In his case, he recounts, the station always operated with a military censor on hand. The challenge was to outwit the censor through codes understood by listeners and through other devices. The best shield turned out to be to say what you wanted to say as if quoting from someone else. His station was closed four times; paradoxically it was always able to reopen after applying to the courts. (He notes that Chileans are very law-abiding people even under a dictatorship.) He believes that his station—whose audience at the time of the plebiscite was two million— became the most important media force leading ultimately to Pinochet's downfall, through heavy use of public opinion polls. It was this station that persuaded the authorities conducting the plebiscite to release the "no" vote result, thereby certifying the end. He is discouraged now by his listeners' shift in interest away from politics and human rights issues toward music and sports.

Though some may applaud the reticence of the post-Pinochet press, many others view the weakened condition of the mass media as a sad and dangerous situation. The media were important for the overthrow, they confirm, but they are even more needed now. One young leader of the Social Democratic party in Congress lamented that even though the military regime lasted only 17 years, a significant proportion of the population nevertheless has no experience of the functioning of a legislature. There is a crying need for widespread political adult education. He thinks that the press does an exceptionally bad job of enlightening citizens about issues before Congress; people must depend on the "soundbite of the day" on television. Thus neither the proper role of Congress in a democracy nor the policy options before it are well understood by the public. How, he asks, can democracy survive in such conditions? The media have a responsibility, which they currently ignore, to help revive the crippled Chilean civic culture.

A senior figure in the Alwyn administration claimed that media coverage of public affairs is not only weak, but skewed in unusual ways. In general the media are only subtly hostile to the government, exhibiting their enmity through misrepresentation and distortion rather then open attacks. Ironically, he finds that—perhaps because of what he describes as their authoritarian training—leaders of the media for the most part treat the president fairly and responsibly. They respect the office if not the incumbent. But media still do not cover government and public policy issues with any depth of knowledge or sophistication. They depend for their information mainly on exchanges with the official press spokesman. They reserve much of their contempt for Congress, whose role in government they simply cannot comprehend. They are only just learning that controversy on policy issues can occur without extreme polarization and conflict. Since 1990 they have maintained that consensus must be the social objective; it may take them until late in the decade to learn that constructive debate is an integral function of full democracy and that dispassionate analysis of policy alternatives is a legitimate and indeed essential role for the media to play.

Rather then take on the powerful family-controlled daily press, the Alwyn government in its media policy has set out mainly to reform television. A new law describes television channels as public property, to be distributed not as a means of political control or in reward for political favors but rather on condition of performance in the public interest. License renewals are scheduled every 25 years, after a performance audit by the National Television Council (NTC), whose members will be nominated by the president for eight-year terms and confirmed by the Senate. Already in operation, though for only a few months at the time of our visit, NTC is headed by a distinguished scholar of politics and the media and is just beginning to implement its charge, which includes encouraging programs of great public interest and discouraging those which contravene accepted social values. The council has powers over both public and private channels and may publicly rebuke, fine or even suspend malefactors. It has been encouraged to conduct research as a basis for regulation and is moving slowly before taking action.

With a staff of only 25, NTC faces a daunting task. Most issues must be approached from scratch. In 1992, for example, one question addressed was whether the owner of a television franchise could sell the concession, or whether it should revert to the state. Concentration of ownership and market power is an ever-present concern, and one criterion for the distribution of channels is to increase diversity and competition. Just how NTC is to fulfill its responsibility to protect decency and family values is another complex question. At least one television channel, operated by the Catholic Church, offers programming that thoroughly explores the moral implications of national and international news.

The government newspaper *La Nación* has an anomalous position under the Alwyn administration. It was a propaganda tool of the Pinochet regime and would thus seem an ideal candidate for privatization. Confronted with a largely hostile press in the private sector, the Alwyn government has preferred to retain *La Nación* as an independent voice in the print media analogous to public radio and television. By all accounts the paper's quality has improved dramatically since 1990. A strong new team of professional journalists has been brought in and coverage presents a wide range of opinions, even including some criticism of government policies and practices. *La Nación* depends heavily on official advertising and government printing contracts for its revenue but intends to build greater circulation and seek private advertising in due course. Ultimately the management hopes the paper will assume a role as "the alternative press," a complement but not a rival to *El Mercurio*, breaking even financially with no public subsidy. This notion of a public-service newspaper, analogous to public radio and television, has not yet been seriously developed. *La Nación*'s experiment should attract world-wide interest.

The Media in the Social Context

Of course, the media are not alone in having to adjust to stability after a period of dictatorship and turbulent succession. Other segments of society that interact with the media have to learn new relationships as well. One senior corporate executive described how under the dictatorship his company's external relationships were very simple: they were solely with the presidential palace. Now he feels a need to inform Congress, educate voters and influence regulators. This is all very complex. He finds himself ill-equipped for these tasks and has been appointing staff and developing special relationships to get the job done. Thus far he has not found the media very useful— reporters do not understand markets and the economy and they cannot make the case for free enterprise effectively. He has been exploring instead techniques of direct contact with various constituencies.

Another very senior and prominent businessman was especially eloquent describing the change in thinking that he himself was currently undergoing. He began by saying that in his view one of the most serious of the "disappeared" during the Latin American military regimes had been the free press. Most citizens have forgotten the proper functions of the media, while the journalists themselves cannot cope with independence. Journalism is still indistinguishable from politics. If a journalist writes a critical story or even asks a penetrating question, it is assumed that this must be for political reasons. No one thinks of professional reasons for journalistic curiosity. Businessmen have traditionally operated with maximum secrecy and have run from reporters. It will take years for them to learn to run in the other direction— toward the reporters—and to accept that reporting in the style of *The Economist* is really good for the economy and the public. The data from the business community must come if democracy and the free market are to flourish. He and most of his business colleagues are immensely relieved at the moderate course of the transition thus far. He suspects that the environment may be the policy area where a democracy today is most in need of journalistic sophistication and expertise. The stakes are becoming very high, and a mistaken environmental policy may easily kill business, or kill a lot of citizens.

Conclusion

Many dispassionate observers think that the most serious challenge to the Chilean media is to retain a balance while returning to the central functions of media in a free society. The media lived through 17 years when they were virtually gagged and then a three-year period of internal division and confrontation. Following a moment in 1990 when the whole society stared into the jaws of tyranny once again and withdrew in horror, the mass media is now developing a new relationship with a society that walks on eggs. The media must discover a *modus operandi* that is true to their principles but that does not break the eggshells. The various media must overcome the backwardness that results from two decades of inactivity and learn to criticize not only "the enemy" but their friends and supporters as well. In due course the media must modulate their deference to power in all forms—in government, the Church, the military and the economy. They must develop an investigative capacity not only on human rights, where their attention now understandably rests, but on the economy, on the environment, on international affairs and on political performance.

The Media in Mexico: Playing Modernization Catchup

The Place of the Media in Mexican History

Paradoxically, among all the four countries we visited, the mass media in Mexico have been the least effective in contributing to democratic change. As one observer rather colorfully put it, "Instead of serving as the locomotive of change, the media have been the caboose of the state." With some conspicuous exceptions, the print media in Mexico are weak, demoralized and heavily dependent on government—"managed," as the tactful felicitously say. Ownership and control of the broadcast media are concentrated in relatively few hands. Despite these conditions there is much ferment about the proper role of the media, both within and outside its publications and productions. And both within and outside government there seems to be a wide consensus that change is coming. The main questions relate to how, when and what.[3]

Relations between government and the media have been close ever since the revolution of 1910, when the modern "liberal authoritarian" state and the single political party, the Institutional Revolutionary Party (PRI), emerged. There are two prevailing perspectives upon this relationship. One is that in the face of inexorable pressures, both internal and external, Mexican society settled sensibly upon a "cooperative" mode of self-government that required a high degree of economic and social control. This led to a one-party government; fundamental change was provided for only through presidential successions every six years. The system was analogous to "governments of national unity" common in many democracies during wartime, in which discussion is permitted within limits but unconstrained criticism is prohibited as a source of faction and dissension. The distinctive rationale in the Mexican case was that the constrained democracy that required this benevolent authoritarianism was expected to function for the long-term and thus required structures that could endure over time. Instead of the propaganda and censorship organs that operate in most countries during wartime, a softer and more flexible set of controls was put in place. This interpretation stresses the well-intentioned and public-spirited motivation of those in authority. Their objective was not personal gain but rather the achievement of public purpose through what they perceived to be the best means at hand. They did not adopt a Western style of democracy because they thought that Mexico could not thus meet the challenges before it. Recently, reflecting their characteristic pragmatism, they have reevaluated the virtues of a liberal democracy and are prepared to accept it in part if not yet *in toto*.

The alternative interpretation of Mexican political history is more cynical. It argues in effect that political leaders since the revolution have been as selfish and venal as those in any other authoritarian regime. They have perpetuated the myth of continuing crisis so as to justify a systematic pillaging of their country and its people. And indeed the Mexican oligarchy has devised as complete and successful a rationale for extraction of economic rents as can be found. They have recognized the centrality of the media as a key agent of control and will not release it unless absolutely compelled to do so. They have depended on self-censorship and indirect rule, but the effect has been the same as that of the most rigorous despotism.

These two perspectives are not of course stark alternatives, and both may help to explain the present scene. Whichever explanation is personally espoused, everyone seems to agree that the last decade has witnessed important change—in the economic sphere toward private ownership and freer markets and in the political sphere toward at least some of the features of a conventional liberal democracy. Partisans of the first perspective see this evolution as reflecting the political elite's sensitive and patriotic response to changing conditions, particularly in recognizing that much might be gained from closer integration with the world economy. Critics, on the other hand, say that the political elite have not welcomed these changes, which have been made only under the pressure of events, especially the serious recession of the 1980s, and only with great (if subtle) resistance.

Both versions would account for the degradation of the media, one as the necessary infringement of conventional press freedoms for a greater good, the other as suppression of a critical force that might impede the process of social exploitation. One observer pointed out that both explanations might be true alternatively: "The government has an angel and a devil speaking to it. The angel says clean up the mess in the media. The devil says leave it for others." Ironically, he notes, much of the rising popularity of opposition to the ruling PRI in recent years may be simply a consequence of the media's own weak critical scrutiny of the opposition. Incompetence may flourish in the shade that would wither quickly under bright sunshine. Those in authority are just now beginning to appreciate the political principle that the triumph of rationality in public life requires effective mass media. The confident modernizers now sense that their own standing may improve and the opposition's decline if given fair coverage by sophisticated media.

The Means of Government Control

No matter which interpretation of recent Mexican political history one accepts, it is indisputable that the Mexican media in this century have experienced sustained and destructive intervention by the state in at least four forms. First, government at several levels and at various times has taken direct action against different media segments whose products they dislike. The results have been complex and the consequences unpredictable. For example, in 1976 the government saw fit to purge the influential daily *Excelsior* of excessively critical elements.[4] The paper was indeed much weakened by the purge, but the offending "elements" in turn proceeded to found three new voices of critical opinion: the magazine *Proceso*, the newspaper *Uno Más Uno*, and some years later the newspaper *La Jornada*. Some thus view the 1976 purge as ultimately counterproductive to PRI's aims. Others, by contrast, see in this a clever trick to remove strong critics from a mass-circulation medium by relocating them to small periodicals read mainly by already disaffected elites. In either case, this highly visible punishment sent a strong message to other journalists of strong critical intent. There have also been repeated charges, not easily documented, that repression of the media in the province, far from Mexico City, has in some cases been more severe, to the point of kidnapping and murder.

The second form of governmental intervention has been pressure exerted on owners of the media through various devices that affect profitability and in some cases, prospects for survival.[5] The most subtle of these operate through the distribution of "advertising" and through payments for publicity (for example, for the petroleum monopoly Pemex or for tourism in one of the states) and for publishing news reports that reflect approved government positions (such as upbeat reports on a foreign trip by a government official).

The magnitude of payments for these officially supplied news items (called *gacetillas*) is quite startling: in some cases, we were told, they may reach $30,000 to $40,000 (US) for several crucial paragraphs. One daily paper with a true circulation of only about 5,000 reportedly has an annual income of about $4 million, presumably in the main from public sources. The rules governing these transactions are rather intricate. *Gacetillas* with a by-line can be more expensive than those without. The intended audiences for planted stories may be varied; for example, a state-level government official may try such means to enhance his prospects for promotion.

The corrupting impact of this system should not be taken lightly. Payments such as those for *gacetillas* have a variety of effects: they blur the lines between journalism and propaganda; they nurture media dependency on public subsidies;and ironically, because advertising payments are not related directly to circulation, they create incentives for reduction in the size and spread of media to minimize costs that are unrelated to revenue. Different media concerns have handled receipt of government payments differently. Some simply do what they are asked and pocket the cash; others insist that some kind of code, such as italic type, identify for their readers all material inserted for the government. Some owners hang their heads in shame; others justify the payments as recognition of the cultural importance of the mass media, analogous to that of schools and art museums. Thus it is difficult confidently to determine the degree of dependency caused by government subsidies. Clearly that is related to the proportion subsidies bear to total revenue. But many observers say that many publications would close if public subsidies were suddenly dropped.

Another financial control on owners and management—in this case, primarily of print media—is exerted through PIPSA, a government paper-distributing company. This monopolistic concern wields its power through sales at below-market prices, below-market rates for finance charges, and minimal storage fees. Until recently media could not purchase paper directly from abroad without a permit and were very tangibly dependent on PIPSA; in extreme cases PIPSA could and did boycott uncooperative "customers." Use of PIPSA to control the press has declined markedly in recent years, perhaps in appreciation of its heavyhanded style. The continuing support for PIPSA among many editors and publishers is evidence of yet another dependency on the cost savings of interventionist practice.

The third form of government intervention is through various kinds of payments made directly to media employees—most notably reporters but also editors, anchors, producers and others—and bypassing publishers and owners. In their most blatant form these payments consist of cash in envelopes ("tokens of appreciation," the infamous *embute* or *chayote*) distributed at news conferences and on other occasions. More subtle manifestations include commissions on sale of advertisements of as much as 15 percent to reporters who cover the advertiser; payment of expenses; assistance in performance of journalistic functions; subsidized housing; and other similarly lucrative favors. Each government agency has its own constituency of dependent reporters. In most cases payments to individual journalists are not part of any grand governmental strategy; usually they are made by individual politicians to promote themselves, their interests or their friends—a practice tolerated within the political culture. Yet one reporter recalled that until recently presidential visits abroad had traditionally been a happy occasion for the attendant media, as the office of the president paid all expenses and journalists had much time for shopping and sightseeing because most of the copy was prepared by the presidential press office for dispatch home to Mexico. (This largesse reportedly ceased in 1992.)

Because payments from government are so entrenched and regularized, many reporters are now heavily dependent on them and could not survive on their salaries alone. Journalists who accept payments seem to rationalize them rather in the way that some medieval Schoolmen philosophically justified the taking of interest in business transactions—on the grounds that the transfer is proffered voluntarily and is not solicited. In this sense, one is not engaged in bribery or corruption but is merely the beneficiary of a magnanimous gesture! It appears that media organized as cooperatives are especially susceptible to corruption, as they lack a strong centralized mechanism for imposing a moral code.

The fourth method of government intervention in the media is through distribution of scarce television channels and radio frequencies only to "politically correct" recipients. This device may serve to control not only the broadcast media but also print media in cases where print owners wish access to television or radio, either as a business venture or as desirable outlets for information products.

In addition the Mexican government has to some extent operated its own media such as the official newspaper *El National*, as well as radio and television stations, in competition with the private sector. But these have been far less effective devices for exerting influence than the four more subtle and persuasive means discussed above. Moreover these government-run media, like so much else in the public sector, today face the cold prospect of privatization.

Because government controls over the media are so widely recognized and accepted, terms like bribes, payoffs, scandal and corruption of the system do not seem quite appropriate to describe the situation. Indeed it is the system itself, not corruption of it, that leads to the degradation. And that governmental control and intervention effectively demoralizes and debilitates the media cannot be questioned. The effects may not be as dramatic as in more uncompromisingly totalitarian regimes, where censorship and cruel repression of journalists are a way of life, but they are not very different. The self-censorship that prevails in Mexico is regulated by relatively large carrots and relatively small sticks; things would not change much if the carrot got smaller and the stick got bigger. The impact in Mexico is probably less on what is said than on what is not said.

The Face of the Mexican Media Today

The consequences of government intervention and control over the media in Mexico are in some respects more complex than those in a conventional authoritarian system. One result of dependency has been a general weakening of the media, especially the print sector. By and large the media are held in low esteem by their consumers and are seen as both inefficient and mercenary. There are few daily papers with much strength or distinction, and there are no weekly magazines with large circulations. Many of the largest papers other than *Excelsior* or *El Universal* (such as *Esto*, *La Prensa* and *Ovaciones*) contain mainly sports, crime reports and local ads. True circulation statistics remain a controversial issue. One observer has estimated that whereas the 25 Mexico City dailies, serving a population of around 20 million, report circulation of three million, the real figure is about 750,000.[6] Another thinks the truth is lower still. Recently an Institute to Verify the Media was created to compile audited data.

Some of the Mexican media are very advanced technologically. For example, *El Sol*, a national newspaper chain, transmits material by satellite throughout the country in the manner of *USA Today*, *The New York Times*, and the *Wall Street Journal*. It is widely conceded, however, that if support from government were to cease and a larger reading public were not quickly attracted, many of the print media in Mexico would be unsustainable and would collapse. On the other hand, observers say, if a truly first-rate paper were to be published, it would sweep the field in a matter of months and increase the field at the same time.

The reading, viewing and listening public is generally cynical about news reportage, and although there is little evidence of open repression of the media, consumers assume bias. One result of this climate of suspicion is that the Mexican populace has not developed the habit of newspaper reading. One commentator said, "The elite read magazines, the rest read nothing." Subtle codes of conduct have evolved for the media and are well understood by everyone involved. For example, while vigorous controversy is tolerated, even encouraged, on some topics like foreign policy and the current economic liberalization in progress, other topics—among them the church, educational reform, military activities and "common moral values"—must be addressed with great caution. The "spin" given to sensitive topics is often more carefully controlled than the content. If there is a demonstration, reportage will play down any violence that occurs. Political rallies for opposition candidates must be shown to have low attendance. Some topics, such as the personal affairs of the president and his family, are simply off-limits.

The absence of vigorous journalistic debate on many subjects means that competition does not contribute to quality control in those areas. One observer remarked, "Too many people write about too many things they know nothing about." Presumably this is as it is intended to be. A distinctive vice of the noncompetitive press is the practice of publishing anything so long as one has "a source," no matter how mistaken or unreliable the source may be. Stories have appeared, for example, claiming that the United States is stealing Mexican rain clouds and is purchasing Mexican children for organ transplants—the evidence being simply that somebody said so. No one felt any obligation to print complementary commentary from skeptics that might enable readers to arrive at balanced truth. Sensationalism reigns unconstrained. One observer stated the problem succinctly: "As restrictions have been lifted on freedom of the press, no ethic of responsibility has been cultivated to match the newfound climate of opportunity." Another, employed by one of the largest papers, admitted that what his paper published was based primarily on press releases and gossip, seldom on hard fact.

One feature that distinguishes the Mexican media scene from what might be expected in a conventional authoritarian state is the acknowledged presence of a few small publications that take critical stands on public policies. These are not *samizdat* papers, persecuted by the authorities; indeed they often receive the same kind of public assistance that their more servile compatriots enjoy. They are distinctive in being willing to bite the hand that feeds them. This category includes both the weekly newsmagazine *Proceso* and the financial publication *El Financiero*. Cynics view these publications as relatively harmless gadflies, tolerated by the political establishment only to legitimize a claim of press freedom to the international community. Optimists, on the other hand, see them as an important nodal point for positive change, the yeast required ultimately to leaven the lump.

Change in the relationship between government and the media is a hot topic in Mexico today. The rationales for change are mainly two: on the one hand, that a modern democracy—to which status Mexico aspires—requires a vigorous free press and mass media; on the other, that free markets and efficiency in the public sector point away from the relationships of the past. And indeed some evidence indicates that payments and subsidies of various kinds have recently been reduced and even stopped (sometimes to the anguish of longstanding recipients), and plans for more cutbacks are under discussion. Some suggest that the most powerful force for change in the relationship between government and the media comes from the "modernizers": high-level liberal bureaucrats (at cabinet rank and just below) who have lived and studied abroad and have experienced the role of a free press in a democracy. Occasionally these "technocrats" or "technopols" (to use John Williamson's most recent term)[7] persuade themselves that political and social change must follow fundamental economic reform—the media can wait. But more often they are annoyed that the mass media do not—perhaps cannot—reflect the progress of the economy. In most cases they are less certain about how to achieve "progress" in the media than in other industrial sectors, where the benefits of competition are more straightforward and output is more easily defined. The true test of their commitment to change lies just ahead. Mexican authorities have long been accustomed to respect, restraint and even complicity from the media. Whether they are prepared to accept and tolerate the skepticism and abuse that the press often heaps upon leaders in a modern democracy remains to be seen.

Most involved with the media in Mexico today avowedly yearn for change, for an end to dependency and for the strengthening of all institutions that will contribute to democratic life. Yet they are clearly uneasy about the process of change. Media owners and employees alike have become dependent on public subsidies. They recognize that competition in the marketplace may bring uncertain rewards, perhaps even none at all. Government for its part is uneasy about whether it can control the pace of social change with modern media in full cry.

The Broadcast Media

Although the press in the nation's center of power, Mexico City, has a powerful influence on national issues, Mexico essentially has no national press. Perhaps as few as 5,000 issues of any Mexico City newspaper are sold in other cities—mainly in Guadalajara and Monterrey. Radio also remains local or regional in its coverage. Television instead is the only truly national medium. Televisa, similar to Brazil's TV Globo in both national dominance and international projection, has a regular audience estimated at 20 million—compared to eight million newspaper readers nationwide (if we may trust our total from published circulation figures). Televisa captures about 92 percent of the national audience during AAA hours (prime time, 7:00 P.M. to midnight).[8]

Although Mexico has deregulated and liberalized most industrial sectors, even including the strategic oil industry, television seems to be one of the few where little has been done to increase domestic competitiveness and open the market to competitors from abroad. Televisa itself, a major industrial conglomerate, includes not only most of the country's television stations but also radio stations, as well as the production and export of television programs, publication of newspapers, books and magazines, publicity and entertainment agencies, real estate agencies, the main cable television network, movie and music production agencies, cultural foundations, museums and tourist agencies.

Until very recently dominant political forces did not consider the broadcast media, and television in particular, a major instrument for creating consensus, nor did political parties use television as a major means for political competition. While not acknowledging a political role, Televisa usually has tacitly aligned itself with the government. A recent analysis of Televisa's political role by Trejo Delarbe, with particular attention to whether newscasts give disproportionate coverage to PRI, the official party, and close doors to the opposition, found that *24 Horas*, Televisa's most popular newscast, devoted only a small fraction of its time (17.31 percent) to covering the 1988 presidential elections. Of that segment, 69.62 percent dealt with the PRI campaign; only 14.36 percent covered all the opposition parties combined. This however compared quite favorably with the alternative newscast, *Da a Da* (produced by the government television channel), which devoted only 12.3 percent of its time to electoral issues; 88.32 percent of that coverage went to PRI, only 4.89 percent to all opposition parties.

Interestingly, radio is an unexpected bright spot in the Mexican media. Its growing popularity among the elite may be linked to the rise of the automobile and traffic problems. Mexico City commuters are captive for hours every morning and evening. They pass the time that might have been spent reading newspapers listening to radio instead. Because radio is mainly local and aired live, any form of effective censorship or control is extremely difficult to impose. As one broadcaster told us: "You ask a good question, and he [the interviewee] just answers. You don't have the opportunity to reflect on whether this might displease some [government] minister." Another commentator praised radio's "bouncy and energetic" ambience and suggested it might be capable of compelling reform in the other media. Others claimed, however, that as radio has become more influential with the populace, government has increasingly attempted to manipulate it through distribution of frequencies to compliant owners and operators.

The audio/video media depend critically on the federal government via the Directorate of Radio, Television and Cinema (RTC) in the Interior Ministry, which allocates concessions (and renewals) for transmission over Mexican airwaves, which by constitutional law belong to the nation. RTC enjoys a high degree of discretion in making decisions, and those decisions cannot be appealed—except, of course, to the president. One recent incident that reveals its power involved a major figure in Mexican journalism who was host of a popular radio program. According to his account, the owners of the radio station were pressed by RTC to terminate the program. The owners instead asked him to file with them an advance list of persons he wished to invite to his program, for prior approval. He considered this an infringement of his freedom of speech and a threat to his professional integrity, and resigned from the station. In the weeks that followed, many other journalists disclosed similar cases in which radio stations had been pressed by the government to give air time to commentators less openly critical, to the exclusion of others known to be vocal against the government or favorable to the opposition.

Is This Truly a Time for Change?

Despite a discouraging history of reform to date, signs of forward movement are presently considerable. Outright payments to reporters seem on their way out, now an embarrassment to payer and payee alike. Government agencies are evidently issuing constraining regulations on payoffs and reducing budget lines for such expenditures. Individual media are breaking with dependency in various ways. At one paper we visited, reporters are instructed to continue to accept payments—but to turn them in to the management, which will reimburse the government source via a company check. In a landmark action in 1992, the Office of the President announced that it would thenceforth issue no indirect contributions or direct payments to the media. The implicit justification for this change was austerity and economy in government, but it seems more likely that the international spotlight on NAFTA made conformity with behavioral norms for public servants in a modern democracy a consideration. Perhaps it is a necessary consequence of Mexican political culture that such a fundamental development as the creation of independent media must be undertaken piecemeal in this way, without vigorous public debate or a resolute declaration of broad policy reversal. More dangerously, through this absence of public, self-conscious reflection these moves toward a free press may be as easily reversed, and as quickly as they were promulgated.

Because constraints on the media in Mexico have been very subtle and complex, their removal may be almost imperceptible. One senses that the media exert pressures from time to time simply to test where flexibility might exist. Since the late 1970s restraints have been relaxed on both editorials and op-ed pieces. News reporting appears to be the last bastion of control. This may reflect a tactical judgment by government controllers about what matters most politically, or be simply an observation that editorials and op-eds are little read or heeded by people who matter. Opposition politicians remain convinced that continuing government influence over news reporting will mean continuing difficulties with achieving balanced coverage in the media.

An interesting natural corrective may be at work in government control of radio, where public subsidies and payments for public advertising have never been as important as commercial advertising. Because private-sector advertising depends heavily on ratings, and because stations find that ratings rise with candid discussions of the news and controversial public issues, they have been increasingly willing to sacrifice public revenues in return for market-based rewards. Indeed some broadcast stations may need to adapt to this new-found freedom more prudently and learn to resist the temptation to present outrageous news reports as a means of swelling their listening and viewing audiences. Several commentators called for better training to increase professionalism in the broadcast media and to improve appreciation for "the relationship between media and power." One critic describes many radio stations today as biased and irresponsible, though not corrupt.

There are at least as many optimists as pessimists about the future of the Mexican media. Optimists believe that the media still trail behind the rest of Mexican society in the present era of change. But events and circumstances will inevitably push the media to catch up: movies, television, NAFTA, increased foreign travel and international exposure will all eventually make laggard media into an embarrassment, potentially unsustainable in the Mexican mass market. Mexican society is generally becoming more demanding and one strong demand may soon be for free and effective media. Public funding for the media is bound to decline over the next years, leading to a beneficial shakeout in the industry and in the profession; the most efficient firms and most competent journalists will triumph. Optimists further claim that enough admirable institutional and individual role models already exist among the media to set high standards for all. One well-informed observer, when pressed, estimated that Mexico might have 20 excellent columnists writing today, and perhaps 100 first-class reporters. In other words, there is a sound base for the development of a respectable profession.

Even one of our most pessimistic informants about the prospects for autonomous reform, in either the government or the media, conceded that through an interaction between the two a bright future just might still lie ahead. The democratizing state will demand more independence in the media, then this increasingly more independent media will demand a more democratic state, then the democratic state better media, and so on. An editor of one of the major Mexico City papers concluded that "the nation's media are just not as good as its people. They deserve better." He found this to be an intolerable situation and unsustainable. Another journalist remarked that "while the media usually reflect the society of which they are a part, in Mexico the media are anachronistic and a step behind." The media missed in 1988 "the moment of chaos, in which society changed directions." But their moment may arrive soon! Those in government who believe that modernization must come first, then a free press, may be about to learn that you cannot have one without the other.

Pessimists about the prospects for improvement in the Mexican media believe that the current condition has deep cultural roots in an authoritarian tradition that will take generations to change. They believe that Mexicans have the media they want and deserve. They deny that present practices are merely anachronistic, rear-guard policies of an obsolete PRI. Indeed they claim that if opposition parties were to gain power these practices would probably continue unchanged, but with different sets of winners and losers. Pessimists see little real progress over the past two decades. The new freedom allowed to columnists and editorial writers, they say, is only a reflection of their ineffectiveness and irrelevance: the columns convey much gossip but little real information or deep analysis. Even the *El Norte* phenomenon (discussed below) is dismissed as a fragment of U.S. culture that has drifted south of the border, like the *maquiladoras* (cross-border assembly plants), and poses no serious threat to the dominant authoritarian mainstream of Mexican culture. One pessimist stated flatly that "the last institution to become democratic in Mexico will be the media."

A spokesman on media affairs who is close to the president in Los Piños ("The Pines," equivalent to the U.S. White House) is one of the most articulate optimists about the prospects for reform of the media. He predicts radical modernization in the media and in their relationship to government as well. He thinks that ideally the media should act as a bridge between government and society, as their name implies, with information flowing in both directions. He admits that perfecting this relationship will take time. Attitudes change slowly, and neither side has yet arrived at well-formulated norms or ethical codes. He insists, however, that the president has already taken important steps to reduce dependency and will do more. Demands for change are increasing and resistance to them is decreasing. Only the most retrograde politicians still think that the old ways are necessarily best. He looks forward to a national debate in the coming years over the role of the media in society, after which he hopes the media may match the reforms that have been occurring in government and the economy. The media, he says, must "catch the rhythm of change" present elsewhere in society.

Inspiration from the North

One of the most exciting developments in the mass media anywhere in Latin America today has been the rise of the daily newspaper *El Norte* in Monterrey, the vibrant industrial capital city of the northern Mexican state of Nuevo León. A few cynics dismiss *El Norte* as merely another unwanted incursion of U.S. corporate culture and style. Most others see it as a phenomenon of wide importance for Mexico and the entire region.

The owners of *El Norte*, the Junco family of Monterrey, created the present paper out of a small regional daily, established in 1938, that looked very much like dailies in cities of comparable size across the country. The current publisher, Alejandro Junco de la Vega, attributes the transformation to his experience and that of his brother Rodolfo as students at the University of Texas at Austin, where they were exposed on a regular basis to American journalism of a high standard. They returned home committed to reforming the family paper and to creating a model for the nation. Today *El Norte* stands in stark contrast to most of Mexico's other newspapers. It operates from a handsome modern building in downtown Monterrey, with the most luxurious appointments and up-to-date equipment and services. The staff is unusually young and well-trained; morale and standards of accomplishment are high. The paper accepts no government-subsidized news stories (*gacetillas*) and remains independent of government advertisers, the largest of which provides only 2.3 percent of advertising revenue. *El Norte* stresses the importance of independence and accuracy in news reporting. The editor quips, "We want journalism with nouns rather than merely adjectives." *El Norte*'s owners see newspapers as only one part of a larger social communications network. Through a partner company they provide to subscribers an on-line service of market-related data.

The story of *El Norte*'s metamorphosis is well known in Mexico and throughout Latin America. Alejandro Junco de la Vega explains that he was determined to build a first-rate paper by accumulating an accomplished staff of journalists with excellent skills and the highest possible ethical standards. When he first started, he soon discovered that most journalists at the time were intellectuals of various stripes, frustrated lawyers, amateur psychologists and such, who lacked any set of common journalistic skills and values. These people, he concluded, could not become the basis for his new enterprise. He wanted a staff that he could pay well and demand much of. Even the raw material for such a staff was extremely difficult to find in Mexico. Schools of journalism and communications were not turning out products he could easily retrain. Most of those who had already settled in with other papers were corrupted by prevailing practices. Thus *El Norte* began its own training program, which today attracts approximately 500 applicants from around the country, from whom 15 are accepted without charge for a six-week course that concentrates on two subjects: how to write for a newspaper, and journalistic ethics. At the conclusion, usually four or five graduates are offered appointments by *El Norte* at salaries not far below those of their U.S. counterparts. The remaining graduates are quickly snapped up by other papers. Virtually all of the current staff at *El Norte* came to the paper by this route. For a number of years a professor from a U.S. school of journalism ran the training program. Now it is directed by a senior Mexican staff member, a graduate of the program herself and former Nieman Fellow at Harvard University. *El Norte*'s management encourages and supports continuing education for staff journalists in a variety of fields.

A central tenet of journalistic ethics at *El Norte* is that conflicts of interest of any sort are strictly impermissible, and unauthorized acceptance of funds from any external source will bring immediate dismissal. Instructions are: "Don't accept even a Coke. Just say no to presents." Thus far only three people have been dismissed. Veteran staff members report that they have developed a virtually Pavlovian negative response to corruption. One mentioned being swept by revulsion when, on assignment, he was offered two chickens!

El Norte's paid circulation is now 140,000 to 170,000 on weekdays, around 300,000 on weekends, plus another 45,000 for the afternoon tabloid. This circulation is probably the limit of opportunity in Nuevo León. One observer compared the paper in its present status to the *Houston Chronicle*, a compliment indeed, but reflective of a regional orientation. Ten other dailies also publish in Monterrey, with a total Sunday circulation of perhaps 600,000 to 700,000, a volume around half that of Mexico City, which is disproportionately larger. Most observers credit the example of *El Norte* and the effective competition it provides for the strength of the Monterrey press overall.

One of *El Norte*'s most distinctive characteristics is its unwillingness to rest upon the status quo. Currently the entire journalistic world in Mexico is agog at the prospect that a new daily national newspaper, entitled *Reforma* and patterned roughly on the *El Norte* model, will soon be launched in Mexico City. To put it mildly, this could inspire a nationwide journalistic revolution. The plan is to bring to Mexico City *El Norte*'s skill in operating a paper with efficiency and integrity, access to overseas news, market data and advertising revenues. Following now familiar practice, a small *El Norte* team from Monterrey has trained a cohort of journalists for the Mexico City paper. By early in 1993 they had received 750 applications and appointed approximately 100 professional journalists. *El Norte*'s leadership is very conscious that their practices have already changed journalism in Mexico, both by example and through competition. But the prospect is for much more change. The challenge is to create an equally distinguished paper for a very different public, in Mexico City, that claims to want *The New York Times* or *Le Monde* but has never been exposed to either.

Alejandro Junco de la Vega describes the media in Mexico today as a hodgepodge in which truth is seldom clear and the role of press freedom is barely appreciated. Bearing upon the media, he says, are history, politics, business and social change. Meddling by people in government, who have never had to produce anything for a market, has caused further confusion, corruption, conflict of interest and lack of direction. Not surprisingly the media have lost their way. Another deep-seated problem, he believes, are public attitudes toward information. Only gradually will the Mexican people realize that free access to information is required for both democracy and efficient markets— and what that might entail. Many public servants continue to suppress information, even such simple data as interest rates at treasury bill auctions. Others simply regard public information as proprietary: one judge even proposed that he should hold copyright to his legal opinions and decrees! The legitimacy of access to information is as important to a free society as freedom of expression. And only free societies can compete in the modern world; "How can Mexico take part in NAFTA with bandages over its eyes? You can't improve your appearance without a mirror. Yet the Mexican instinct has been to break the mirror." Capitalist vices flower in secrecy; a free market system simply cannot survive without the means to enlighten the darkness. Mexico has a plethora of policy questions ahead: What exchange rate regime to adopt? How much public infrastructure to retain? How much privatization to effect? If told that government alone is best equipped to answer such questions without public input, the people should recall that the proclaimed liberators are at the same time their old enslavers.

Alejandro Junco de la Vega appreciates that if the new national paper in Mexico City is a success, the *El Norte* model will have a far greater impact than it already has achieved to date. This new paper will not only siphon readers away from the existing broad array of small papers but may attract new members to the reading public and capitalize on the growth of informed interest among middle-class elites involved in the modernization under way throughout society. Junco de la Vega is convinced that the small readership for newspapers in Mexico City persists because existing papers have been written mainly to please government sponsors rather than those who buy them. A large latent demand lies open and untapped.

The management of *El Norte* do not give the impression that they think they have all the answers. Their journey south to Mexico City is a great adventure. They worry in particular about how to build up, and quickly, cadres of reporters and columnists with special skills in substantive areas of urgent national policy concern such as the economy and the environment. They have concluded that it is probably easier to turn an economist or an environmentalist into a journalist than vice versa—but attracting such experts to a journalistic career in Mexico may not be easy.

Another issue that concerns *El Norte* is how best to reflect within its pages (in Monterrey and Mexico City alike) opinion from the intellectual community in addition to news and editorial expression. Traditionally, Mexican papers have tended to reflect one or another ideological position, and independent commentators in their pages take predictable positions. *El Norte* has rejected this strategy in favor of a smorgasbord of outside contributions, none of which the paper endorses implicitly or explicitly. Only through such eclectic confrontation, its founders and staff believe, can those who really understand issues be identified and charlatans distinguished from serious students of public affairs.

El Norte is certainly not without critics within Mexico. The most vigorous charge is that it is merely a reflection of American capitalism and is now an alien creature in the Mexican landscape. Defenders respond indignantly that it is indeed northern in style, but "not à la Texas, à la Monterrey. It is what *regiomontaros* (residents of Monterrey) like and buy." Critics contend that it is gray, commercial and responsive only to market pressures from readers and advertisers. It lacks the pungency of newspapers based on the European model. It has no soul. It is part of the movement, represented by NAFTA, that would homogenize all of North America and make Mexico the 51st state. These critics want *Le Monde* and lament that in *El Norte* they are getting the *Miami Herald*. At the same time they concede that newspapers in the modern world must depend either on government or on the market. Those that seek a third way, like *Le Monde*, are in financial trouble. Mexico's experience in the 20th century causes even some of these critics, when pressed, to prefer the market to government.

In more specific terms one scholar of communication who has studied *El Norte*'s coverage of one important news incident in some detail argues that the paper is not in fact as far removed from the traditional culture of Mexican journalism as it professes. He claims that, like the other Mexican papers, *El Norte*'s reporters tend not to explore news stories from the perspectives of the poor, radical leaders or small-business persons. Too often they accept the official version as authoritative. An ingrained respect for authority still impedes their search for information inconsistent with official doctrine. He found the paper's editorial comment completely unconstrained, but the news reporting—which is what really counts in the eyes of the government—merely "respectable." Overall highly complimentary of *El Norte*'s accomplishments, he is uneasy that this single model might sweep the field. He calls for "a plurality of voices" in news gathering and a willingness to entertain seemingly implausible explanations and "unreliable" sources. He blames the American influence substantially for keeping *El Norte* "too respectable"—a posture, he believes, that limits the paper's effectiveness in investigative reporting, in contrast, say, to *Proceso*.

The Road Ahead

The central questions confronting the mass media in Mexico today are whether change is truly in progress and whether the constructive forces are strong enough to lead change in a positive direction. After a lifetime of disappointment, many foresee nothing but gloom. As two visitors from abroad, however, we came away with considerable optimism. That economic, political and social evolution is now occurring throughout the media no one can deny. Key institutions like political parties, trade unions and the church are in different forms of crisis and are no longer performing their traditional functions.

People at all levels are now compelled to reach out for new forms of communication and for means to participate in the change already under way, for a voice and for the space in which to explore and discuss the events that affect their lives. The mass media offer various opportunities to meet these demands.

That many of Mexico's mass media institutions today are antiquated, obsolete and anachronistic also cannot be denied. Heavyhanded government intervention is yet omnipresent, even while influential leaders in government express unease about the quality of the media. Most of the print media remain weak, backward and dependent. The broadcast media evidence unhealthy concentrations of power. The profession of journalism is demoralized and unable to come to grips collectively with the ethical and professional issues that face it.

The two forces for change that most impress the outsider are citizens' insistent demands for reform and the existence of strong models on which to build. Citizen demands are visible at several levels. Sophisticated intellectuals and political elites complain that they have few credible and effective means by which to communicate. Individual newspapers or magazines have very limited strength and credibility and find it difficult to reach an influential audience effectively or to generate a measured and informed debate. Moreover they are tired of being manipulated. The broad middle class, in turn, finds it difficult to rely consistently on any of the media for reliable presentation and interpretation of the news. In response they vote with their feet, purchasing few copies of any print medium. The poorer classes, facing the breakup of familiar political parties and of traditional links with government agencies, trade unions and the church, are reaching out to the media—especially radio and television—as never before. (We heard many accounts of householders' telephoning talk-show hosts at moments of crisis before calling the police or the water department.)

Amid these increasing demands for reform, some models for change are already in place. The most impressive is *El Norte*, a modern, effective high-principled newspaper of the kind found in most developed industrialized nations. Its projected publication of a new national newspaper, based in Mexico City, is one of the most exciting developments in recent years. If successful, the consequences can only be beneficial. Several other publications likewise afford admirable models for professional emulation, notably *El Economísta* and a few other regional papers such as *Diario de Yucatán*.

In addition to these promising models in the private sector, government is also undertaking policy change that is likely to alter the face of the media.

Reduction of public subsidies through formerly condoned *gacetillas*, *chayotes* and subsidized raw paper sales is likely to prompt a shakeout, from which only the strongest and most economically viable media organs will survive at an economically defensible scale. Government is contributing directly to this rationalization by privatization of media that it holds and operates directly.

What Mexico seems to lack at present is a pointed, well-informed national debate over the future of the media. The crucial issues still need to be defined and clearly presented, with arguments effectively stated on all sides. It is striking that modernizers in government, who proclaim clear vision of a free-market economy and a somewhat hazier view of a liberal democracy, seem not to have formed any perception at all of the press and mass media in the Mexico of the 21st century. What sympathetic outsiders can perhaps contribute more than anything else is the opportunity for participants in a future debate to focus on the right issues, build up a detailed understanding of them, prepare their arguments and take a position of independence from which to express their views. How this opportunity can best be provided is discussed in the remaining chapters of this report.[9]

An Assembly of Themes

One of the objectives of this monograph is to explore areas of media and communications policy where the four countries examined may have common concerns, among themselves and with other countries as well. Some of these concerns are specific to emerging democracies, but many are of widespread relevance. We now draw together some of the threads from the four preceding chapters to see how these countries' experiences can be compared and to discern whether further opportunities are at hand for cooperative and collaborative investigation.

What follows does not imply that the U.S.'s rather mature democracy has already reached satisfactory answers to all the questions identified, or that answers can be provided at all without first specifying social norms in each particular country and investigating cause-and-effect relationships more precisely than anyone has been able to do to date. Nevertheless even this brief survey has yielded a hearty menu of prospects for training, research and debate.

At a high level of abstraction, public policy regarding the media and communications can be stated in a way that elicits wide agreement. Virtually everyone, for example, is prepared to favor a strong and free press, broad access to information and a well-informed citizenry. It is only when generalities are reduced to particulars that uncertainties and disagreements become apparent. The remainder of this chapter reviews some central questions that emerged during our inquiry, on issues that have been addressed differently within the four countries and over time, in the hope that comparative analysis and a reduction to essential principles may yield some general conclusions that could illuminate policy formation everywhere. Our list is far from exhaustive, and should be seen as merely illustrative of a much larger set of interrelated questions.

Government and the Media

High above all other questions related to the media in these four countries and throughout Latin America is what the proper relationship might be between media and government.[10] At one extreme it is clear that too close involvement is potentially destructive to both, as indeed can be seen in numerous instances. It is now widely apparent that a democratic government cannot thrive without effective media in the proper juxtaposition to it. The media must be there to provide facts and interpretation to the interested citizenry. And where some of the organs of the state, such as the legislature and the courts, are not performing effectively as checks and balances to the executive, the media must be there to fill in as the "loyal opposition."

In none of the four countries has government worked through to anyone's satisfaction the question of the right distance to be maintained between the executive branch of government and the media. In fact at one time or another in each of these countries the executive has been prepared to coopt the media, thereby removing the distance entirely, and to constrain the media from transgressing various special interests. At present the Mexican media are probably the most effectively controlled and denatured, through a complex set of government policies that operate via the carrot of bribery, combined with the stick of occasional punishment for what are perceived as hostile acts. In Chile a national culture of caution and conservatism infects the media, putting off the day when they may vigorously confront authority. In Argentina a small "vanguard press" wrestle with a strong president, like David with Goliath, while the rest of the media and government opposition mainly look on. In Brazil the media rejoice in having wrought the downfall of a venal president, yet it remains ultimately unclear whether this is entirely to their credit or whether they were used as instruments by ruling elites.

Although media that are muzzled by government certainly cannot perform their essential role in a democracy, the other side of the issue presents an equally difficult question: whether entirely unfettered media can be consistent with all stages of political development, most especially during transition from an authoritarian regime. There is no shortage of informed and experienced voices, both within and without the media, that claim that only totally uninhib-

ited media can do their job legitimately, that all constraints on absolute freedom are illegitimate and doomed to do more harm than good. This is prima
facie a persuasive argument, but it needs to be probed and tested against
historical cases.

Thus we might begin with some questions regarding freedom, discretion
and regulation.

- What form and amount of information should flow from government to
  the media? What is the proper function of the press release? Should
  there be regular "background" briefings?
- What should be the role of the "spokespersons" in government, speaking for the president, ministers, departments and other units of government? Is there a cost to democracy as well as a benefit to governmental
  efficiency in this kind of channeling of news?
- What should be the limits of the public's (and therefore the media's)
  right to know? If freedom of information is not absolute, what are the
  correct principles to guide this constraint? Obviously current governmental operating files cannot all be open for public scrutiny, yet they
  should not be sealed beyond the point where demonstrable public
  damage will clearly follow from openness. How can a policy of maximum
  reasonable access be implemented?
- How and to what extent should media be regulated by government?
  At which level of government should regulation occur? Federal? State?
  Municipal? Through which branches of government? The president?
  Executive departments? The legislature? The courts? What degree of
  discretionary authority should the executive branch of government
  retain under legislation, especially toward the broadcast media?

Economics of the Media

Like it or not, in any free society the media are engaged primarily in economic
activity in one way or another. Newspapers, magazines and radio and television stations are producers and distributors of goods and services to readers
and listeners. Suppliers meet demanders in markets of a certain kind. And
the suppliers must make a profit! Even nonprofit media must at least answer
to budgets if they are to stay afloat.

Market analysis alone certainly will not illuminate all such questions that arise
regarding the media, but it may go part of the way. Some of the questions
that economists might ask include the following:

- What is the nature of the goods that media produce? Is there a need for government to have some role in their production and sale? Most of the output of both print and broadcast media consists of "private" goods with few "externalities," that is, these are goods whose costs are incurred mainly by the suppliers and whose benefits are received by the demanders. When someone buys and reads the comics section of the newspaper, the purchase price will reflect, on the one hand, the enjoyment experienced by the purchaser and, on the other, the costs incurred by the newspaper for type, ink, labor time, royalties to the artists, etc. But some of a medium's output may also be in the nature of a "public good," yielding benefits to society as well as to consumers.

- If left to private exchange alone, a public good is underproduced. Precisely what are truly public goods, yielding positive externalities and deserving of public subsidy, sooner or later becomes a debatable matter of judgment. One criterion for such judgments might be the educational accomplishments of the media; in this sense their public benefits would be analogous to those that arise from public schools. Another criterion might be cultural, whereby benefits would be analogous to the externalities of museums and selected theatrical and musical performances. During transitions to democracy, the public benefits from media may depend on how effectively they inform citizens about changing circumstances and the opportunities open ahead. But these criteria are observations in theory. Can they be clothed with empirical reality? In such circumstances, is it possible to identify actual and potential products of media that generate "external benefits" to society beyond benefits that accrue to purchasers? How?

- Who should own the media? Because of the media's distinctive role as producers of public goods and services, the pattern of ownership is of particular significance, even apart from issues of market concentration (discussed below).

- Should the media be privately or publicly owned? For the production of goods that warrant heavy public subsidy, an argument obviously exists for public ownership and operation. And indeed the four countries we visited offered many examples of public ownership in all branches of the media. Yet many of these instances evinced problems of efficiency, incentives, patronage, principal-agent relationships (such as managers in pursuit of their own interest rather than the public interest) and old-fashioned corruption. Whether those problems arise substantially from monopolistic market conditions and would be reduced by competition is not clear.

- A related question is the concentration of ownership in the hands of a few individuals, families, special interests, regions or social classes. Is this concentration necessarily a barrier to democratization, such that parts of society inevitably feel (correctly or not) that they are effectively barred from access to the media and social communication by inhospitable owners? Will this problem disappear if that concentration of market power is dissolved? Is the problem especially intense when owners acquire several media in one market (for instance, several newspapers)? Or several media of different kinds (such as newspapers and television stations)?

- Should government intervene to encourage competition in media markets? When markets contain too few firms to assure competition, production tends to be too low and selling price too high. To increase consumer welfare, government in such cases may require that large firms break up to increase competition, or regulate the industry to make it produce and sell at levels that approximate the competitive norm. Such tactics are often adopted toward "public utilities" such as electric power and telephone services, and sometimes for major manufacturing sectors such as automobiles and steel. Should the media be systematically submitted to antitrust action? Would a solution to economic problems of concentration also solve some of the social and political problems discussed above?

- How should "economic rents" from the distribution (for private use) of scarce public communications resources be allocated? A distinctive feature of the broadcast media is that they require access to resources in limited supply that are traditionally possessed and controlled by the state: television channels and radio frequencies. To retain for public purposes the economic rents that flow to these resources, these channels and frequencies should be allocated either by auction or by some recognized criterion of subsidy in return for the provision of public goods. Since the rents accruing to these scarce resources typically rise over time, their auction or alternative (re)allocation should be repeated at intervals. Would such periodic (re)auctions also serve to reduce the political and social corruption that currently prevails through existing methods of allocation?

- What other forms of governmental intervention into media markets are necessary or tolerable? The histories of the four countries we visited are rife with examples of various interventions, ostensibly for benevolent purposes but in reality so as to increase media dependency; low-interest loans, bribed workers, subsidized owners through advertising and other devices, influenced trade-union behavior, rationed transportation and affected prices and quantities in other ways. Is it possible that clear specification of when government intervention in media markets is legitimate would constrain illegitimate interference?

■ What should be done to assist "public interest programming"? The "public goods" aspect of media products was mentioned above. How can the public subsidy required for the assurance of such goods be allocated without inviting political corruption and market distortions? Models from more mature democracies, such as the British Broadcasting Corporation (BBC) of the Corporation for Public Broadcasting (CPB) in the United States, might prove illuminating.

Investigative Reporting

One of the most dramatic and exciting functions of the media in an emerging democracy is to explore the accomplishments of public and private institutions according to accepted standards of behavior and performance.[11] Especially where other organs of society that perform a watchdog role are ineffective, paralyzed or corrupt, this function can be enormously important. Media can root out evidence of corruption, identify inefficiencies and expose conflicts of interest to public view. The activities of individual media, even single reporters, may assume heroic character from the mysteries probed and the magnitude of the powers that are challenged. Presidents may be toppled by revelation of their untoward actions, corporations irretrievably damaged and reputations destroyed. Fame, fortune and international prizes may accrue to media that investigate such leads successfully. And various and severe social costs may befall those who abuse the privilege. Careful attention to policy questions related to this topic may help retain the benefits and reduce the costs of investigative journalism:

■ Investigations of public and private performance have long been carried out in civilized societies by the courts, by legislative committees, by nongovernmental organizations and by auditing units of various kinds. These bodies have all developed rules and practices that protect the rights both of those being investigated and of members of the public who have a right to know. Especially in circumstances where the investigative role of the media takes on exceptional significance because other monitoring forces are weak, should comparable rules be devised to assure the credibility and responsibility of journalistic investigators?

- More particularly, can laws against libel and slander be structured to enable the media to perform their investigative function without restraints, yet keep them mindful of the costs of injuring innocent persons and institutions in the process?

- And should investigative reporters receive obligatory (credentialed) instruction in such matters as how to unearth reliable sources, how to present material fairly and rules of evidence?

Investigative journalism is clearly a powerful weapon against those who would subvert either the political democracy or the competitive market system. But at present it is also a blunt instrument that badly needs some refinement. Many observers of democratic transitions in Latin America, and indeed of political reform in the United States, think of investigation by the media as a sacred trust that at times alone has kept the barbarians beyond the gate— or kicked them back outside. And of course they are right. But an equally strong case can be made, for the long run at least, that the investigative art requires careful scrutiny and perfection in form. Badly applied or in excess, it can misdirect public opinion.

Strengthening the Coverage of Critical Policy Areas

Closely related to investigative reporting are questions about how the media may keep well informed about increasingly complex and technical public policy issues.[12] No country on earth has solved this problem to perfection, but some have made substantial progress in these areas. This is clearly a case where a good deal may be learned from comparative study. As with the other areas, innumerable questions arise:

- What kinds of special training can be arranged to produce journalists who are both professionally competent and technically proficient in areas that they may be called upon to report on, such as the economy, education, the environment, health, human rights, urban affairs, national security and international affairs? Can universities be persuaded to think creatively in order to attract excellent students to demanding and stimulating programs that will truly generate dual expertise in journalism and in a substantive field of specialization?

- How can avenues be created and sustained that will keep journalists continually in touch with authorities in their areas of coverage? (Organizations like, say, the Council on Foreign Relations and the Institute for International Economics, which perform that function in the United States and actively include journalists in their discussions and policy reviews.) Can universities be encouraged not only to train specialized journalists but also to sustain them while they practice? What parts of universities are best suited to this purpose? Schools of communications? Public policy programs? Departments in the social sciences? New units entirely?

- How can journalists become included systematically in communities of specialists in various policy-relevant areas, so that over time they will be able to cover policy discussions from the perspective of participant insiders, rather than as "science reporters" invited in from outside as an afterthought? Where is the borderline at which they might become too comfortably "inside"?

- Should there exist, in any democracy, systematic means whereby media specialists in critical policy areas may occasionally be supported in their own in-depth research on important problems? In this they may discover the limitations as well as the power of policy research. If such support is desirable, how should it be funded?

- Is it practical to think of building and sustaining international networks among journalistic specialists in important policy areas, on the grounds that there is at least as much in common across national borders as there is unique within a nation? Could this be accomplished best through existing organizations like the InterAmerican Press Association and the International Press Institute or through new institutions of some kind?

The Profession of Journalism

Is journalism a profession, an occupation or a trade?[13] Those who make their living from the media in Latin American tend to be divided over whether they are simply employees responding to the demands of employers, or professionals with principles, standards and formalized codes of conduct, or independent thinkers enlisted ad hoc for particular expertise and/or personal acuity. Questions that arise in discussions of journalism as a profession revolve mainly around whether journalists have an obligation to resist the pressures around them and perform certain functions inherent in their calling. Do they, for example, have a responsibility to lead, rather than always to follow their audience? Should they press always for standards that are higher than those that prevail at the moment? Should they remain pure in a sea of corruption?

Regardless of credentials and employment history, one distinctive occupational hazard for journalists is that they are importuned continually and variously by individuals and groups that wish the contents of the media to reflect particular self-interested viewpoints. In addition to influence from owners, publishers, managers and editors of the media for which they work, not to mention the government, they frequently encounter pressures from advertisers, the church and other guardians of community values. One primary reason to advocate professionalization of journalists is to reinforce and reward their resolve to remain independent of such forces. They have a responsibility transcending self-interest to resist interference from both negative and positive forces, to stand up to terror and bigotry and to reject blandishments of all kinds. Another compelling reason is to help journalists understand and instantly recognize conflicts between journalistic principle and their own short-run individual interests. Whether the apparent prevalence of in-house and personal conflicts of interest, especially in Argentina and Mexico, is the result of ingrained cultural traditions in the society at large or of particular institutional "cultures" of the moment is unclear. Regardless, the establishment of strong professional standards is one sure way of reducing the problem.

By way of summary and conclusion we notice that "rights and responsibilities" are a much-discussed topic in Latin America today. Although that debate might be mistaken as a unanimous call for media freedom, it is usually rather the reverse. Journalists, it is asserted, must ethically consider the consequences of their endeavors and, for example, not report, publish or unduly pursue a story if the social outcome is likely to be negative on balance. Is this a practical or desirable course to follow? The obvious danger is that this doctrine may be used to criticize and oppress the media by claiming that they have ignored or neglected their responsibilities to tell the truth and to freedom of the press. The counteranalogy used to defend this doctrine—that free speech does not justify a cry of fire in a crowded theater—has some legitimacy, but how much?

Experience of authoritarian rule in recent history has brought the media in each of the four countries we visited to uneasy balances between these two poles of freedom and discretion, usually with great sensitivity to what political, social and personal realities can sustain. In this respect of seeking and testing balances, they are not so different from their colleagues worldwide. But their perceptions of the balance occur at an exceptionally important juncture for the future of the societies they serve. For this they both deserve professional standing and need the insurance of professional standards.

The Quest for Expertise and Values: U.S.-Based Training Programs for the Latin American Media

Prior chapters have analyzed in some detail the various issues and troubles that confront those engaged in providing print and broadcast media to four prominent Latin American countries: Argentina, Brazil, Chile, and Mexico. Distinctive socioeconomic settings have influenced what is expected of journalists in each of these societies, the degree to which they remain controlled by governmental and corporate structures, the influence of regional particularities within each country, and the strengths and weaknesses of media contributions to the public policy debate within respective polities. Since World War II and especially in the past ten to 15 years, numerous training programs have been established by U.S.-based institutions that afford members of the Latin American media diverse opportunities for honing their technical journalistic skills and for reflecting on characteristics in historically democratic societies that might apply to their own circumstances. These programs, sponsored by a wide variety of institutions throughout the United States, fall generally into three categories.

First are a very large number of graduate-level degree programs at U.S. colleges and universities that lead to the master's degree in journalism, mass and organizational communications, and radio, television and film. Many of these programs have been in operation for decades. The 1993 *Peterson's Guide to Graduate Programs in the Humanities and Social Sciences* lists 86 U.S. programs that lead to an advanced degree in journalism, 76 programs in mass and organizational communication, and 86 in radio, television, and film. Notable examples in major state universities include programs at the University of Michigan, the University of Missouri at Columbia, the University of North Carolina at Chapel Hill and the University of Texas at Austin. Programs at significant private universities are listed for Boston University, Columbia University, New York University, Northwestern University, the University of Southern California, Syracuse University and Washington University in St. Louis. Still others are offered at highly respected smaller institutions such as Emerson College and the New School for Social Research. For the most part these programs are open to students of all backgrounds and are not especially geared to Latin American media specialists. When the Institute of International Education needs to place foreign nationals in U.S. graduate degree programs in journalism and related fields, it readily contacts more than 20 institutions particularly interested in receiving non-U.S. applicants.

A second category are university-based fellowship programs tailored especially for midcareer media specialists, including those from Latin America, but which do not lead to an advanced degree. These tend to expose the fellowship recipient to an array of techniques and value questions prevalent in contemporary American journalism but generally do not provide an exposure to the practical realities of daily life in the newsroom. These fellowship programs are often limited to a single semester or academic year, and the recipient is awarded a certificate upon completion of the program, rather than a degree.

A third category are specialized programs established by independent organizations affiliated with the mass media that emphasize on-the-job training or advanced seminars for the working journalist. These programs may last from several days to several months, and some have been developed with the Latin American journalist expressly in mind. Here too, those who complete the program receive a certificate.

Given the breadth and heterogeneity of these offerings, we cannot hope to provide a comprehensive evaluation here of the entire array of opportunities in the United States that are open to guests from the Latin American media. Instead we highlight eight programs that represent different approaches, and summarize their main characteristics. These summaries, more descriptive than evaluative, are intended to suggest the range of options available. (We have deliberately emphasized categories 2 and 3.) After that, we make some general observations on their value to the working journalist from south of the Rio Grande.

1. The Inter American Press Association

The Inter American Press Association (IAPA) is the oldest and most widely known U.S.-based organization that promotes contacts with Latin American journalists. Housed in a modest suite of offices in northwest Miami, it generates a tremendous number of programs with a full-time staff of only seven. IAPA was established in 1942 "to defend and promote the right of the peoples of the Americas to be fully and freely informed through an independent and responsible press." Another stated purpose was "to further understanding and friendship in the Western Hemisphere." IAPA has always been distinguished by two characteristics: its inter-American representation and governance, and its independence from government support. From its beginnings the organization has been led by prominent publishers and editors of the printed press from Canada to South America. Having this backing has meant that IAPA has enjoyed reasonably substantial financial support to carry out its programs and numbers among its members some of the most important journalistic figures in the hemisphere. Some of the journalists with whom we conferred viewed it as an establishment organization that is sometimes risk-averse and unwilling to tackle subjects of limited interest to its powerful membership. But despite these occasional reservations it is widely agreed that IAPA has consistently defended freedom of expression by journalists throughout the hemisphere and that this remains the cornerstone of its activities.

IAPA has refused to accept support for any of its projects from any government in the Western Hemisphere, thus retaining credibility in the eyes of those who view with suspicion government support for any organization related to the press. It relies instead on contributions from its members and also raises considerable sums from major foundations, especially in recent years from the Knight Ridder Foundation and The Freedom Forum. Over the years key American publishers and editors from the *Miami Herald*, the Scripps-Howard Newspapers, *The New York Times*, and indeed most of the major American newspapers and newspaper chains have been associated with IAPA. Since the mid-1980s its executive director has been Bill Williamson. Williamson has had a varied career, at one time teaching journalism at Memphis State University and then spending a long stint in Brazil, where he was a key figure in the Rio and São Paulo Chambers of Commerce and with the English-language daily *Brazil Herald*. At present IAPA's president is Alejandro Junco de La Vega of *El Norte* in Monterrey, Mexico; first vice-president is A. Roy Megarry of the *Toronto Globe and Mail*. A 20-person board of directors provides oversight of membership and policy issues; for 1992-95 the board numbers, besides Megarry, six Americans (including representatives from the *Miami Herald* and the *Wall Street Journal*), two from Mexico, three from Central America, one from the Caribbean, and seven from South America. A 32-member Advisory Council, which has enlisted many senior figures such as Andrew Heiskell, formerly of *Time* magazine, and Julio Cesar de Mesquita of *O Estado de São Paulo*, provides programmatic advice on an ad hoc basis. This multinational composition seems more acceptable to some Latin American journalists who would feel uncomfortable in a program run by a purely U.S. organization.

Membership in IAPA falls into several categories. Newspapers of general circulation and magazines published at least six times yearly are eligible for active membership and are represented at membership meetings by their proprietors, publishers, editors, editorial directors or managers. Annual membership dues are based on a sliding scale according to the member publication's circulation, from $130 for those with less than 5,000 to $1,300 for those with circulation in excess of 250,000. There are separate fee structures and regulations for corporate members, news agencies, associate members, teachers of journalism and syndicated columnists.

Over the years IAPA has established three major programs:

The IAPA Scholarship Fund. The first of these programs, the IAPA Scholarship Fund (founded in 1954), offers from three to 18 scholarships each year, depending upon the applicant pool and funding sources. These scholarships are aimed at individuals who are working journalists or journalism school seniors or graduates between the ages of 21 and 35. They enable Latin American and Caribbean scholars to apply for admission to a U.S. or Canadian university with a recognized journalism school; recipients must attend classes for a full academic year. U.S. and Canadian scholars may in turn select a Latin American or Caribbean country in which to study and work; recipients must take a minimum of three university courses and submit a major research project paper at the end of the academic year. U.S. and Canadian scholars receive $10,000 plus health insurance. Latin American scholars receive the same plus round-trip air fare.

In its first 25 years, the Fund awarded 259 scholarships to North Americans, Latin Americans and West Indians totaling more than $750,000. Well over 100 additional scholarships have been awarded since. The Fund was established with an initial gift from John S. Knight and in its formative years received support from the Knight Foundation, Copley Charities, The New York Times Foundation, the Reader's Digest Foundation, Scripps-Howard Newspapers and Time, Inc. During the first 25 years donations to support the Fund ranged from $20 from a former scholarship winner to an $80,000 endowment from the Robert R. McCormick Charitable Trust. Most of the gifts came from newspapers or newspaper foundations, with major exceptions being grants from the Tinker Foundation and the Bacardi Corporation. More recently a major contributor has been the Angel Ramos Fund, named after the publisher of *El Mundo* in Puerto Rico.

Although there has been no systematic evaluation of how recipients of the scholarships have since fared, anecdotal evidence collected by IAPA in a 25-year report cites a number of consequences. It was often noted that the prestige of the scholarship had enhanced recipients' upward mobility in their careers. On returning home many received promotions in-house or moved on to excellent new positions elsewhere. A number of the North American recipients emphasized how much the scholarship had aided their understanding of Latin American culture, increased their appreciation of the role of the press in Latin American societies and honed their Spanish or Portuguese language skills. Latin American recipients, on the other hand, cited enhanced knowledge of the techniques of journalism: layout, photojournalism, copy editing. Several also became associated with or founded schools of journalism modeled in part on the institution in North America where they had studied.

The Technical Center. A second major component of IAPA is its Technical Center, which has been directed since the early 1980s by Dr. Julio Muñoz, a Chilean national who holds a doctorate in communications from the University of Minnesota. The Center has its own officers and executive committee; the chairman of its board of directors is Luís Fernando Santos of *El Tiempo* in Bogota, Colombia. It primarily conducts seminars in Latin America that speak to the needs and interests of Latin American publications. One recent program, held in Colombia jointly with the McDill School of Journalism of Northwestern University, was addressed to analysis of cost and revenue data and drew top managers of the Latin American press. A major achievement of this seminar was the sharing of sensitive data among the many publications represented and an exchange of perspectives on how the cost data were analyzed and fed into management decisions.

In the spring of 1993 the Technical Center sponsored a seminar in Santiago, Chile, to establish the Inter American Press Institute of Investigative Reporting. The seminar attracted more than 100 participants from 12 countries and brought together a team of experienced investigative journalists who shared their personal experiences and work methods. Speakers included Andres Oppenheimer, author of *Castro's Final Hours* and member of a *Miami Herald* team that was awarded a Pulitzer Prize for investigative reporting; Horacio Verbitsky of *Page Twelve* in Buenos Aires; and Geraldo Reyes, editor of *El Nuevo Herald* in Miami and president of the new Institute. The seminar included discussions of the ethics of investigative journalism and of corruption in Latin America. The new Institute expects to publish a bi-monthly newsletter and to disseminate transcripts of the twice-yearly symposia it plans to sponsor.

The Technical Center has also sponsored symposia on issues of relevance to Central American publications and on a wide variety of other matters. It normally sponsors more than a dozen programs in Latin America annually, ranging from newsroom technology to computer skills to techniques of photo-journalism. Financial support is made available to smaller, regional publications so that their representatives can attend the symposia. Attendance at seminars ranges from 25 to 80; the Center thus involves about 400 individuals annually in its on-site practical workshops.

The Technical Center also administers the IAPA Press Institute, modeled on the American Press Institute (API) that serves U.S. and Canadian newspapers. The IAPA Press Institute is to be headquartered at API headquarters in Reston, Virginia, and will provide peer-professional training with simultaneous interpretation for newspaper personnel of the region through12 six-day seminars each year. To date Latin American newspapers have pledged $100,000; a further $300,000 is expected from U.S. sources.

The Press Freedom Project. IAPA's third main focus of activity relates most directly to the protection of journalistic freedom of expression throughout the hemisphere. Its new Press Freedom Project, headed by a young Argentinian journalist, Ricardo Trotti, works with a volunteer network that has traditionally provided IAPA with information on abuses of press freedom. One goal has been to extend this network to include reports on abuses of the press in the United States and Canada. (For example, the Project recently identified ardent members of the Cuban-American community who disagreed with the editorial policy of the *Miami Herald* to the point where they destroyed its vending machines and blew the legs off a Cuban-American reporter on the paper's staff.) Trotti also hopes to develop a database on abuses of the press. He estimates that over the past 40 years some 500 journalists have been killed to silence their voices. He has written accounts of recent violations of press freedom in Peru, Chile, Canada and Puerto Rico. IAPA has received a challenge grant from the Knight Foundation to begin this project.

2. The Center for Foreign Journalists

Established only in 1984, the Center for Foreign Journalists (CFJ) has rapidly become the most prominent U.S.-based organization for training and assisting foreign journalists. It characterizes itself as a "full-service professional assistance center for foreign journalists, news managers and their organizations." CFJ conducts practical workshops in the United States and abroad, sponsors seminars on media issues and orientations to the press and broadcast industries, offers consulting services and personnel training for overseas work and publishes and distributes professional "how to" literature and audiovisual aids on advanced journalistic techniques. An independent nonprofit organization with handsome quarters in the American Press Institute building in Reston, Virginia, CFJ is funded by private contributions, grants, and service fees.

CFJ's executive director since its inception has been George Krimsky, who covered Eastern Europe, Russia and the Middle East for the Associated Press for 16 years prior to assuming his present position. By all accounts the Center has also benefited enormously from the leadership and contacts of Tom Winship, former editor of the *Boston Globe*, a co-founder who served as its first president. Founding benefactors included, in addition to Mr. Winship, a distinguished list of journalistic organizations: The Boston Globe Foundation, Cox Enterprises, the Dow Jones Foundation, the Gannett Foundation, The Hearst Corporation, the Knight Foundation, The Robert R. McCormick Charitable Trust, The New York Times Company Foundation, Time, Inc. and the Times Mirror Foundation. CFJ projects have since been sponsored by major philanthropies, including (among many others) The Asia Foundation, the Andrew Mellon Foundation, the Jessie Smith Noyes Foundation, the Rockefeller Foundation, the Ford Foundation and the Xerox Foundation. The Center's annual income, $698,000 by 1989, has continued to grow rapidly (to $1.88 million as of 1992).

Training Activities. In its first eight years of operation CFJ conducted 230 training and education programs for 3,800 journalists, executives, and media officials from 164 countries. Training activities include a course on "basics," ranging from five to 21 days and led by veteran journalists, that focuses on the who, what, when, where, how, why and "so what" of good journalism, through workshops and seminars in basic reporting, basic news writing, basic editing and standards and ethics. Advanced workshops and seminars are offered on in-depth reporting, coverage of issues faced by developing nations, advanced editing and analysis reporting and editorial commentary. There are also workshops and seminars on newsroom administration, financial management, building and holding an audience, newspaper and magazine design and broadcast publishing. These and other programs are staffed by visiting and adjunct faculty recruited among respected journalists and other experts in substantive fields of specialization. The day we visited Reston, the Center was conducting a workshop for visiting Azerbaijani journalists—on how to interview U.S. government officials!

The Knight International Press Fellowship Program. A major new initiative of the Center is the Knight International Press Fellowship Program, supported by a $3 million grant from the John S. and James L. Knight Foundation that was announced in August 1993. The program "will fund a service corps of media professionals who will spend from one to nine months on consulting and training missions at developing news organizations, training centers and universities. While priority will be given initially to Eastern Europe and Russia, other areas of the world, especially Latin America and South Africa, also are prime mission sites." As with most CFJ activities, this new program is intended to highlight both the philosophy and the practice of sound journalism and to emphasize the need to separate news from commentary in journalistic practices.

Latin American Emphases. Because of Krimsky's background in Eastern Europe, Russia and the Middle East, and because IAPA's activities are so well recognized, CFJ chose not to emphasize Latin America in its first years of operation, with the notable exception of environmental reporting. Its overall emphases in the developing world have thus centered on Africa, Southeast Asia and South Asia. One initial judgment of CFJ staff was that in Latin America the "Three R's of journalism—reading, writing and editing" were well understood, and that newspapers there were well funded by oligarchies, governments and political parties. They perceived a far greater need elsewhere in the world.

Nevertheless in 1986 CFJ sought and received a grant from the Jessie Smith Noyes Foundation to conduct workshops in Latin America on environmental reporting. Sessions were held initially in Chile and subsequently in Costa Rica and Venezuela, all in conjunction with local journalistic organizations. All told, CFJ has since conducted more than 50 programs involving Latin American journalists, about 15 percent of its total activity: 19 were orientation sessions held expressly for Latin American journalists, all on environmental reporting; the balance were media training sessions for journalists from a variety of countries, in which at least one Latin American participant was enrolled. (Included in this latter category is an annual session that CFJ hosts for the Alfred Friendly Fellows, discussed below.) Except for the environmental programs, almost all were held in the United States. Most of the nonenvironmental sessions were brief orientations on how the U.S. media think and operate. In addition in July 1993 CFJ completed a review of Latin American media coverage of environmental issues for The Worldwide Fund for Nature.

The report summarizes the strengths and weaknesses of environmental reporting in the region and provides statistical summaries of the communications organizations in each country.

3. The Alfred Friendly Press Fellowship

The Alfred Friendly Press Fellowships are awarded annually to 12 print journalists from developing countries. Unlike the programs sponsored by IAPA and the CFJ, the Friendly Fellowships are focused entirely on an active work experience. Except for a ten-day orientation seminar held in Washington, D.C., recipients spend no time in the classroom or in formal training; each fellow is placed in a single organization (in rare instances, in two) for a five-month work assignment.

The fellowship program was conceived and endowed by Alfred Friendly, who joined the *Washington Post* in 1939, was the paper's managing editor from 1955 through 1966, won a Pulitzer Prize for foreign affairs reporting in 1967, retired in 1971 to write books on the history of the British admiralty and other topics,and established the fellowship program in 1983 shortly before he died. Based first at the Institute of International Education (IIE) and now freestanding, the program has three primary objectives: to provide fellows with experience in reporting, writing and editing that will enhance future professional performance; to enable fellows to gain a practical understanding of the function and significance of the free press in U.S. society; and to foster continuing ties between free-press institutions and journalists in the United States and their counterparts in other countries. It operates from a small suite of offices on Connecticut Avenue in downtown Washington.

Applicants are expected to have an excellent command of written and spoken English, to have completed at least three years' full-time professional experience, to have their employers' endorsement and to have demonstrated commitment to a career in journalism in their home countries. All finalists are given a formal interview. Recipients are all between the ages of 20 and 40, and preference is given to those with limited U.S. experience.

The orientation session each June introduces the new fellows to media technology and journalistic practices prevalent in the United States and also addresses the functions and problems of the free press in U.S. political and social structures. Fellows visit Congress, the State Department and the White House, meet the Washington press corps, and become better acquainted socially. They then proceed to their assigned organizations for five months.

Sponsoring organizations have included the *Atlanta Constitution*, the *Boston Globe*, the *Chicago Tribune*, the *Los Angeles Times*, the *Cleveland Plain Dealer*, the *Baltimore Sun, USA Today* and the *Washington Post*. Usually fellows rotate assignments among different desks (city, foreign, features) to gain a variety of experiences. They attend a midterm reunion in late August in New York City. In December at the end of the term, they reconvene to review their experiences.

With its emphasis on English-language fluency, this program has attracted relatively fewer journalists from Latin American countries than from Anglo-phone countries of the developing world. To date six Latin American and Caribbean countries have been represented—Brazil, Chile, Jamaica, Mexico, Peru and Trinidad—in a total of 35 countries worldwide. In 1987 one of 11 fellows was Latin American; in 1988, three of 12; in 1989, two of 11; in 1991, one of 12; in 1992, one of 11. One typical example of a recent Latin American Friendly Fellow is Maria Filomena, of the class of 1991. Then 30 years old, she was editor of the marketing and management desk at *Gazeta Mercantil* in São Paulo, Brazil. She had worked previously for TV Globo and for *Folha de São Paulo*. She held a bachelor's degree in journalism from a college in São Paulo and had visited the United States previously as a tourist. She spent her fellowship at the *Nashville Tennessean*.

4. The Institute of International Education Journalist Exchange Programs

The Institute of International Education (IIE), founded in 1919, is the largest and most active U.S. nonprofit organization in the field of international educa-tion exchange. It administers education and training programs, including the Fulbright Graduate Scholarships, provides educational advising and testing to students in many countries, conducts and publishes analyses of international student populations in the United States, and convenes conferences and workshops. Its headquarters are in New York City, across from the United Nations Building, and it has offices in Mexico and several other countries.

The Mexican-U.S. Exchange Fellowships. In 1989 IIE initiated a Mexican-U.S. Journalist Exchange to provide opportunities for professional development to journalists in both countries and to promote broader public understanding between the two societies. The five-year program was funded by a major grant from the Ford Foundation as well as by support from The Tinker Founda-tion, Mex-Am Cultural Foundation and other sources. It offered fellowships to enable journalists to sharpen their reporting skills, study key issues in U.S.-Mexican relations, and obtain firsthand knowledge of each other's countries.

From 1989 through 1993, 18 Mexican journalists studied in the United States; the exchanges involved, among various others, representatives from *El Excelsior*, *El Economísta*, *El Norte* and *El Financiero*, who were hosted at *New York* magazine, *Newsday*, the *Journal of Commerce* and the *Baltimore Evening Sun*. Eleven U.S. journalists went to Mexico: representatives from the *Phoenix Gazette*, the *Fort Worth Star-Telegram*, the *Houston Chronicle* and the *El Paso Times*, among others, were placed at publications like *El Universal*, *La Jornada* and *Uno Más Uno*.

Like other fellowship programs described in this report, IIE's exchange program adopted some distinctive features. In this case, recipients were placed with host agencies and worked with colleagues in similar positions for a three-month period. They were free of deadlines and had the time to develop in-depth stories on key issues. (Topics ranged from the environment to economic policy, to migration and border issues, to social and cultural matters.) The program was administered through IIE's New York and Mexico City offices, which handled all recruitment, placement, orientation and monitoring of the fellows.

Like the Friendly Fellows, IIE fellows had to have a minimum of three years' professional experience, a good command of the host country's language, and a demonstrated commitment to a journalistic career. At the end of each fellowship term a week-long workshop was held in New York City to provide an opportunity for the fellows to meet with senior staffers from *The New York Times*, the *Wall Street Journal*, and other major publications and organizations. They also shared their experiences with foundation representatives and IIE trustees and staff and submitted short articles evaluating their experiences and discussing the program's relevance to their career goals and professional development. According to an evaluative review at midpoint in its five-year phase, fellows found the program a useful and rewarding experience. A number were promoted upon return to their home employers; others have since been awarded other prestigious fellowships. Several noted how much they learned about the society in which they had been placed, as well as about the technical details of journalism in the host country.

The five-year program was completed in 1994. But new funding was already being sought to continue it.

The Tri-Lateral Journalist Exchange Fellowships. Recently IIE received a major grant from the Freedom Forum to initiate a Tri-Lateral Journalist Exchange Program. Modeled along the lines of the U.S.-Mexican Exchange, it will enable 12 journalists to work directly with host publications in Canada,

Mexico and the United States, reporting on key issues for their home publications and obtaining first-hand experience in each other's countries. The first class of fellows arrived at host organizations for a three-month term in September 1993 (Mexican and U.S. journalists) and January 1994 (Canadians). As in the bilateral exchange program, fellows continue to receive salaries from their home organizations and write articles for them while being "mentored" by a peer at the host institution. A one-week orientation, a nine- to ten-week hands-on program, and a one-week evaluation workshop at term's end are again the basic structural elements of the program.

5. Selected University-Based Programs

Among the myriad university-based programs, four have been selected for summary that illustrate a range of approaches to the subject of journalistic exchange.

The Nieman Fellowships. Arguably the most prestigious journalism fellowship program in the world, the Nieman Fellows program was established at Harvard University in 1938 through a gift from Agnes Wahl Nieman of Milwaukee, who bequeathed the funds in memory of her husband Lucius, founder and publisher of the *Milwaukee Journal*. After several ideas (such as establishing a school of journalism, or acquiring foreign newspapers on microfilm) were proposed and rejected, it was determined to use the funds for a sabbatical fellowship for experienced journalists.

Walter Lippmann served on the committee that selected the first class, nine fellows each with eight or more years' experience, all between the ages of 26 and 40. Currently there is no age limit, and a typical Nieman class consists of 12 U.S. journalists and ten to 12 colleagues from other countries. Now, in just over half a century, Nieman Fellowships have been awarded to more than 850 journalists from almost every state of the Union and from more than 50 foreign countries. The program is housed in a charming Greek Revival building from 1836 that was remodeled early in the present century to a late Georgian style. Renovated again in 1978, it is now the Walter Lippmann House of the Nieman Foundation and has offices, a reading room and a seminar room for the fellows.

Nieman Fellows nominate their successors. As with age limits, there are no specified educational qualifications (some recipients reportedly did not finish high school). Applicants must be full-time news or editorial employees or photographers with the general-interest media and have a minimum of three years' professional experience (successful candidates usually have at least five to ten years). They must have their employers' consent for a leave of absence for the academic year from September to June. In some cases established free-lance journalists are considered. For foreign journalists, the only additional stated requirement is fluency in spoken and written English. However, the Nieman Foundation is required to use its endowment funds solely to support U.S. fellows; foreign journalists must compete for space available under sponsorship of restricted grants through the Nieman Foundation or by securing funds from other sources.

Nieman Fellows must attest that they will return to their employers at the end of the sabbatical, that they will refrain from professional work during the fellowship period, that they will complete all the work in two academic courses of their choice (one each, in the fall and in the spring semester), and that they will remain in residence in the Cambridge area each term while classes are in session. They receive a stipend for living expenses and are accorded auditing privileges in all Harvard classes. Usually most fellows audit two to four classes each semester, selecting one course for which to complete required work; the instructor of that class then sends a written evaluation of the work to the Nieman office. In addition the Nieman program holds a wide variety of seminars where fellows meet guest speakers from the academic, governmental and journalistic worlds. Each fellow is also affiliated with one of the Harvard residential houses, centers that are the foundation of the university's social structure.

Historically, relatively few Latin American journalists have been Nieman fellows because of the absence of funds. Now, however, a fellowship from the Knight Ridder Foundation routinely supports one Latin American fellow each year. In the 1992-93 academic year, there were in fact six Nieman fellows from Latin America: two each from Argentina, Brazil and Mexico. The Knight Latin American Fellow that year was Francis Pisani, aged 49, a free-lance journalist based in Mexico City who has special interests in U.S.-Latin American history and in the political and economic forces that are creating a new relationship among countries bordering on the Caribbean.

In our discussions with him, Pisani claimed that the greatest benefits of the Nieman program are the time to reflect, the ability to take advantage of the resources of a great university and the interaction with other talented journalists from all over the world. He noted that he had some extra advantages over other Latin Americans in the program because he had a French passport. Although he had lived in Mexico for the past 13 years, he had been a Mexican correspondent for *Le Monde* for four. This gave him a much broader view of journalism than would otherwise have been the case. He believed that seminars at the Nieman Foundation on the ethics of journalism were fascinating but of limited applicability in Mexico, where journalists must deal routinely with self-censorship and death threats. He and other Nieman Fellows with whom we spoke clearly valued the "shop talk" of the Friday luncheons. As one observed, "The way I see the world now is very different. The world was very small before the Nieman."

The Center for International Journalism. The Center for International Journalism at the University of Southern California was founded in 1985 and admitted its first students in 1986. It provides fellowships for experienced journalists and focuses on Latin America as a model for considering problems of reporting in the developing world. Directed by Murray Fromson, formerly a foreign correspondent for the Associated Press and CBS News, the program is 12 months in duration and offers a master's degree or certificate through courses at the university from September until May and through summer courses at El Colegio de Mexico in Mexico City. The summer program includes travel throughout Mexico and a requirement to write four stories for publication.

The program is designed for journalists with a bachelor's degree and at least five years' professional experience. Its goal is to assist working journalists who aspire to careers as foreign correspondents, reporters on foreign policy, editorial writers, international business writers or managers of news policy. The 1991-92 class consisted of 12 fellows from the United States and Mexico. The 1992-93 class drew U.S. participants from major news organizations, including CBS News, the *Chicago Tribune*, the *Los Angeles Times*, the *Miami Herald* and the *Philadelphia Inquirer*. Latin American members arrived from the *Buenos Aires Herald*, *El Economísta*, *El Financiero*, *Imevision*, *La Jornada*, *Notimex* and *El Universal*, all of Mexico City; and *El Norte* of Monterrey. In addition to their summer travel experience in Mexico, the fellows visit the California-Mexico border to meet with key officials on both sides and review immigration, human rights, environmental, agricultural and economic issues. They also take a ten-day spring trip to Washington, D.C., to meet with government officials, various foreign embassies, and think-tank specialists. The Center also sponsors a rich seminar series throughout the year. A recent innovation has been the introduction of the Television News Lab, which allows students in the introductory broadcast classes the opportunity to write, report and produce a weekly newscast that airs over Southern California cable stations. Participants enroll in a variety of courses dealing with American foreign policy, Latin American history, and problems of health, housing, education and nutrition in the third world.

The program has been funded throughout by grants from private foundations; major supporters include (among others) the Carnegie Corporation, the Copley Foundation, the Ford Foundation, and the Hewlett Foundation. The University of Southern California absorbs the Center's administrative and operating expenses and provides a number of teaching assistantships for younger journalists; it also funds the Mexican summer semester. The program's distinguished advisory board includes Carlos Fuentes, Thomas Hughes, Marvin Kalb, Ted Koppel and Judy Woodruff, among others.

The Hubert Humphrey Fellowships. The Hubert Humphrey Fellowship Program was established in 1979 to commemorate the activities of Senator and later Vice-President Humphrey on behalf of third-world economic and social development and the improvement of relations between developing countries and the United States. The program brings accomplished professionals from the developing world, Central and Eastern Europe, and the former Soviet Union to the United States for a year of graduate-level study and related professional experiences. The U.S. Information Services offices and the Fulbright Exchange Commissions overseas nominate fellows, and the J. William Fulbright Foreign Scholarship Board approves the final selection. The program is administered for USIA by the Institute of International Education. It is not a degree program, but those who complete the course successfully are awarded a certificate.

Participating fellows are clustered, according to subject area of specialization, at various U.S. universities. Concentrations have included fellows in agriculture, economic development, educational planning, natural resources, finance and banking, public policy and urban planning. Placements have been arranged at Tulane, Cornell, Boston University, Penn State, American University, Johns Hopkins and the University of Washington, among others. During the 1993-94 academic year a record 188 Humphrey Fellows (including 31 journalists) participated, placed at 15 universities.

The University of Maryland College of Journalism was selected to host a group of Humphrey print journalist as Humphrey Fellows in the fall of 1993 (their broadcast media counterparts were received by Syracuse). In the class of 16 fellows at Maryland we encountered three from Latin America: a freelance writer from Bogota, Colombia; an assistant metropolitan desk editor from *Jornal do Commercio*, Recife, Brazil; and an editorial writer and columnist from La Paz, Bolivia. The program was directed by Ray Hiebert, an academic advisor to the Voice of America on international journalism training programs who has conducted lectures and workshops in 15 African countries. The associated faculty included Gene Roberts, who led the *Philadelphia*

Inquirer to 17 Pulitzer Prizes during his 18 years as its executive editor; he also is presently chair of the American Committee of the International Press Institute and has recently been named deputy editor of *The New York Times*.

The fellows were enrolled primarily in a specialized Humphrey seminar of 28 three-hour sessions, combining American studies and journalistic topics that focused on the U.S. political system, freedom of the press, ethics of the press, media economics and management and selected other issues. In addition the fellows were able to take advantage of the College of Journalism's professional relationships and resources. These include the Capital News Service, in which students at bureaus in Annapolis and Washington cover regional government offices and agencies. The College also has close working relationships with the National Press Club, the American Society of Newspaper Editors and other Washington-based organizations, to which the fellows enjoyed access.

The Duke University Visiting Journalists Program. Each year journalists from around the world spend intervals of several weeks to several months at Duke University under the auspices of the DeWitt Wallace Center for Communications and Journalism and the Terry Sanford Institute of Public Policy. Since its inauguration in 1977 the Visiting Journalists Program has served more than 400 visitors. Latin American participants (usually two each semester) are supported through a grant from the Ford Foundation.

These Latin American Fellows study at Duke University for 14 weeks along with journalists from the United States and a variety of other countries (recent enrollment included representatives from Germany, Poland and Japan). They engage in independent study, participate in the university life, visit off-campus businesses and organizations and travel around the United States. Latin American Fellows have the opportunity to meet regularly with other visiting journalists, learn about the role of media in the United States and study a variety of academic subjects such as political science, public policy, economics, and environmental affairs.

The Latin American Fellowships are designed for journalists with experience in newspapers, magazines or broadcast media. Fellows are expected to attend classes and seminars to further their understanding of political and social issues in the United States and Latin America, including media and public policy. The fellowships also offer opportunities to exchange views and information with other journalists through informal activities and weekly roundtable discussions featuring guest speakers; to pursue substantive interests through lectures and seminars throughout the university; to learn firsthand about U.S. media, society and politics through off-campus visits to print and broadcast institutions, government offices and nongovernmental organizations; and to explore policy issues through Duke University's Terry Sanford Institute of Public Policy. Latin American Fellows are in turn invited to speak to student groups about media, culture and public policies in Latin America. They have full access to Duke's libraries, dining halls and athletic and cultural facilities.

The Net Effects

The training programs reviewed in this chapter illustrate the diverse opportunities through which Latin American media specialists may obtain additional knowledge and exposure to journalistic experience in the United States. In several cases, programs offer a two-way street, whereby interested applicants from the United States and Canada are offered reciprocal opportunities to move south for study and experience. In various ways these programs and fellowships afford participating journalists some key common benefits:

- Time for study and reflection, in university settings, on the role of journalists in a free society, on questions of ethics in journalism and on the rights and responsibilities they have to stimulate the public debate in a democracy.
- Hands-on experience with the craft of modern journalism in newspapers or at radio and television stations, where they can perfect technical skills of writing and editing and learn as well about media technology and management.
- Means to obtain substantive knowledge of subject matter or technique. The former may include training in modern economic analysis, environmental science and policy and other fields that they expect to report on and analyze upon return home. The latter includes the techniques of investigative journalism, which are still in their infancy in much of Latin America.

By all accounts journalists who have been exposed to the study-abroad programs described above have benefited greatly. Certainly many have received promotions or otherwise made a significant advance in their careers. But they have also, more importantly, broadened and deepened their understanding of what they are about, where they fit in their societies, and what contributions they can and should make to the democratization process. We are convinced in general of the merits of each of these programs.

In a previous examination of U.S. study-abroad programs we proffered several basic findings: that study abroad is a dimension of higher education that should be taken into account across the full breadth of educational programs and institutions; that everyone can play; that there are an abundance of ways to go about it; and that, when done well, it is not easy.[14] It seems to us that each of those observations is likewise relevant to the present survey of programs relevant to the Latin American media. Foundation officials and campus leaders must think clearly and innovatively about how to promote linkages with the Latin American journalistic community. If the North American Free Trade Agreement is valuable because, in the end, it will create jobs on both sides of the Rio Grande, then the promotion of a healthy, vigorous and responsible press in Latin America is in the interest of everyone in the hemisphere.

Exposure to the ideas and techniques that such programs afford should not be limited to the working reporter but must be made available to the editor, anchor and publisher as well. Only if the leadership of the media has an appreciation of the value of a democratic press will such learning be properly valued.

The diversity of the programs summarized above indicates that there is no one magic formula. Shorter and longer courses, seminars and internships, programs in the U.S. and in Latin America—all can be of great value.

Finally, the difficulties of participants' experiences cannot be ignored. We know that cultural adjustment is not easy, for short or long periods. We know that Latin American journalists may depart frustrated that they cannot fully apply what has been learned, because circumstances are so very different at home. (*Norteños* too may return from exchange programs with much to ponder.) We know that a certain amount of "aftercare" is required, so that skills and concepts once mastered are not permitted to atrophy. But we also know that the ideas of a free society are contagious and difficult to constrain once learned. Philanthropic, academic and journalistic communities in the United States and internationally can therefore make no wiser investment in the health of the people of our own hemisphere than interacting constructively and creatively with the Latin American media.

Recommendations

Throughout these pages we have suggested, both directly and by implication, actions we think could profitably address the manifold problems and expanding prospects in the Latin American media today. More than anything else, we conclude that this is a time for serious internal reflection and introspection on questions related to the media and communications in the four countries we visited, and probably throughout the region. In this brief closing chapter we list again the topics of greatest urgency, along with some of the modalities that occur to us as ways to deal with them.

Topics for Inquiry

- How can the mass media contribute more effectively to the development of strong and durable democracies across Latin America? How can they successfully and responsibly contribute to the achievement of popular consensus on issues of great contention, and communicate facts and interpretations of facts to all parts of society? How can they help to constrain and correct excesses in democratic institutions when these are not checked or balanced in other ways?
- What should be the precise relationship between government and the media? Is there a need for protection of one from the other? Can the notion of "rights *and* responsibilities" be given substance and precision?
- What should be the economic structure of the media? Is competition truly feasible as a means of constraining abuses of the market? Should there be some constraints on family ownership and control? On multi-

media conglomerates? On vertical and horizontal concentrations? Can the familiar antimonopoly policies of divestiture and regulation be safely employed in the media? How can scarce goods like radio frequencies and television channels best be distributed by the state? What is the case for "public interest" media, either state-operated or state-subsidized?

- What is the nature of the journalistic profession? What are the best forms of training and midcareer enrichment? Are credentials desirable to protect the public from journalistic misbehavior?

- What models from other countries would be most useful in Latin America? Are North American examples becoming too dominant? Should more attention be turned to developments in Europe, whence many of the original models for Latin American journalism in fact came? What can be learned from the experiences of other developing regions, and other regions where authoritarian political regimes have recently been removed?

- What can journalists in the industrialized countries of the Northern Hemisphere learn from inquiries now under way in Latin America? Are the problems being addressed as "live" in the north as in the south? Is the metaphor of "leaders and followers" less valid than a cooperative search for understanding?

Suggested Modalities

We suggest three promising approaches that may be taken toward the topics set forth above. All require funding, but so modest in relation to the consequence of improved understanding that we find the case to be overwhelming for a combination of public and private funding, from the north and from the south—from within Latin America and from its friends in North America and Europe.

- **Institutional Development**
  We believe there should exist throughout the Latin American region a network of strong, independent multidisciplinary research and training institutions devoted to the study of issues related to the media and communication. These might be fully free-standing or attached to universities. They should, however, maintain a suitable distance from the journalistic professions, the communications industry, and the state, as these will constitute their subjects of study. These institutions, in

part for their self-protection, might establish close links with each other across the region and with friendly equivalents in North America and Europe. An important role for private philanthropy worldwide should be to provide sufficient resources to give these institutions the independence they absolutely require.

- **Scholarly and Professional Exchange**
Questions before the media worldwide are sufficiently universal that thoughtful students of problems in one country can learn much from what happens in another. Exchanges of the kind described in the previous chapter have already been of very great value and should be strengthened and sustained. Exchanges within the region should also be increased. In some cases exchanges might be addressed especially to focused training—for example, on investigative reporting, or in such specialized fields as economic policy and environmental policy.

- **Collaborative Investigation and Inquiry**
Not nearly enough advantage has been taken of the challenges that confront the media across the region and beyond. For example, a major international conference could be convened on the topic "Government and the Media in Latin America" that could explore in depth how Latin American governments relate to the print and broadcast media, and identify ways in which greater independence of the media could be acquired, which would strengthen democratic processes in these societies. A mixture of Latin American participants could be invited from the press and from government, along with specialists from North America and Europe, and a "white paper" could be produced recommending how best to strengthen independence of the media given the constraints within various Latin American societies. Similar conferences and collaborative inquiries could be undertaken on the economics of the media and the changing nature of the journalistic profession in Latin America, with special reference to television and radio. Unquestionably the vast majority of Latin Americans receive news about their own societies and the world primarily from the broadcast media, which are themselves undergoing rapid change. A better understanding of how this industry works and how it could be strengthened would be of major assistance in supporting the democratization process throughout the hemisphere.

End notes

1. In the obituary of a prominent American journalist (*Sunday Morning*, 22 August 1993).

2. Bill Hinchberger, a São Paul-based journalist, has published several useful analyses of the Brazilian television scene. See, for example, "Brazil's Media Monopoly," *Multinational Monitor*, January/February 1991, 37-40.

3. Helpful introductions to the economic, political and social change under way in Mexico include Riordan Roett's *Political and Economic Liberalization in Mexico* (Boulder and London: Lynne Rienne, 1993), and especially Luis Rubio's "Economic Reform and Political Change in Mexico," in *Mexico's Alternative Political Futures*, edited by Wayne Cornelius et al. (San Diego: University of California Center for U.S.-Mexico Relations, 1992).

4. The story of the celebrated *Excelsior* purge has been told in two semific-tional accounts by persons closely involved: Vincente Lenaro's *Los Periodis-tas* (The Journalists) (Mexico City: Joaquín Mortiz, 1978) and Hector Aguilar Camín's *La Guerra de Galio* (The War of Galio) (Mexico City: Cal y Arena, 1991).

5. The vast subject of corruption in the Mexican media was discussed by the Mexican journalist Raymundo Riva Palacio in a paper prepared while he was Nieman fellow at Harvard University in 1992: "Mexican Press on the Take? A Case Study of the Mexico City Press" (from a copy in our files).

6. See Riva Palacio, "Mexican Press on the Take?" 33.

7. See John Williamson, "In Search of a Manual for Technopols," *The Politi-cal Economy of Policy Reform* (Washington, D.C.: Institute for International

Economics, 1994) 11, who credits the term to Jorge Dominguez and Richard Feinberg.

8. According to Alan Riding, for many years a *New York Times* correspondent in Mexico, the country has become a nation of television watchers. Even the poor, semiliterate viewers receive the complex stimuli of entertainment programs, advertising and propaganda. Television, in his view, is the primary influence in the cultural, political and economic activities of the general population. See Alan Riding, *Distant Neighbors: A Portrait of the Mexicans* (New York: Random House, 1984), 374-75; there is a Spanish edition: *Vecinos distantes: un retrato de los Mexicanos* (Mexico City: Joaquín Mortiz, 1985).

9. Discussion of issues surrounding television has thus been left rather thin in this chapter, in part because of the difficulty we encountered in persuading anyone to talk about the issues. Our requests for interviews with the dominant organization, Televisa, were all denied. Each person we contacted at Televisa responded that television is an entertainment medium and not relevant to this study—and moreover, that it would be necessary that we talk to a more junior official. Moving down the line, we at last reached someone who said that he was too junior ever to grant interviews!! This was virtually the only failure of cooperation we met with in all the countries visited.

10. This topic is discussed in greater detail in Michael B. Salwer and Bruce Garrison, *Latin American Journalism* (Hillsdale, N.J.: Lawrence Erlbaum Associates, 1991), and Marvin Alisky, *Latin American Media: Guidance and Censorship* (Ames: Iowa State University Press, 1981).

11. This subject is covered very effectively in Peter Benjaminson and David-Anderson, *Investigative Reporting* (Ames: Iowa State University Press, 1990). See also *Television, Politics, and the Transition to Democracy in Latin America*, edited by Thomas Skidmore (Baltimore: The Johns Hopkins University Press, 1993).

12. On this question see Gary Atkins and William Rivers, *Reporting with Understanding* (Ames: Iowa State University Press), and George Tuchman, *Making News: A Study in the Construction of Reality* (New York: The Free Press, 1978).

13. Jim Willis addresses this topic in *The Shadow World: Life between the News Media and Reality* (New York: Praeger, 1991).

14. Craufurd D. Goodwin and Michael Nacht, *Abroad and Beyond* (New York: Cambridge University Press, 1988).

Appendix

Summary of Meeting of Journalism Training Providers and Donors, May 1994

Meeting to discuss and review the IIE research study:
Talking to Themselves: The Search for Rights and Responsibilities of The Press and Mass Media in Four Latin American Nations

by Craufurd Goodwin and Michael Nacht

Institute of International Education, 809 United Nations Plaza—May 17, 1994

Presenters:
Craufurd Goodwin
James B. Duke Professor of Economics
Duke University

Michael Nacht
Dean, School of Public Affairs
University of Maryland

Participants:
Greg Adams
Office of American Republics Affairs
U.S. Information Agency

Philip Arnold, Consultant
International Media Affairs

Bryna Brennan
Director of Journalism
Center for Foreign Journalists

Joan Dassin
Director, Latin American and
Caribbean Programs
Ford Foundation

Lisa Ellis
Executive Director, International Programs
Freedom Forum

Miriam Friedmann
Program Officer, New York Office
Friedrich Ebert Foundation

Mr. Reinhard Keune
Director, New York Office
Friedrich Ebert Foundation

Andrew Radolf
Senior Information Officer
UNCESO Liaison Office with the U.N.

Andrea Taylor
Director, Media Projects
Ford Foundation

Vivian Vahlberg
Director of Journalism Programs
Robert R. McCormick Tribune Foundation

Meeting Report

Opening Remarks by Presenters

Following their introduction by Richard Krasno, President of the Institute of International Education, Craufurd Goodwin and Michael Nacht began the discussion with some opening comments about the research study that they recently completed for IIE, with support from the Ford Foundation. Goodwin described the study as a meditation on the subject of journalism training needs in Latin America, aimed at a broad audience and incorporating a concern for public policy. Research for the study was based upon the authors' observations and analysis as they travelled through Argentina, Brazil, Chile, and Mexico, meeting with and interviewing key journalism figures in each country.

Michael Nacht observed that the countries on which the study focuses reflect the current trend of emergence from authoritarian regimes, thus making the study relevant to the countries of Eastern Europe and the former Soviet Union. Five themes or questions for discussion can be gleaned from the manuscript: the relationship between government and the media, the economics of the media (who owns the media), the role and technique of investigative reporting, the need to strengthen critical policy analysis and the profession of journalism. A number of these issues are addressed successfully through U.S. training programs. In particular, such programs provide journalists with the time and opportunity to study, reflect and expand their international horizons, give them practical, hands-on experience and increase their substantive knowledge. The conclusions of the study focus on several recommendations for journalism training programs:

1. The creation and support of a network of free-standing journalism schools;
2. The maintenance and increase of scholarly and practical exchanges;
3. The establishment of collaborative investigations of universal themes in journalism, such as the economics of the media.

Discussion

The discussion focused on three main areas: cooperation among journalists in Latin America, the profession of journalism in Latin America and the effectiveness of journalism training programs.

Cooperation Among Journalists:
Victor Goldberg, an IIE trustee, began the discussion by noting the advantages of peer contact across geographical boundaries using electronic communications, such as computer networks. He asked whether this might be useful for Latin American journalists. Bryna Brennan, of the Center for Foreign Journalists, said that the technology required for such contact is simply not available uniformly in Latin America. This comment was followed by Craufurd Goodwin's point that one important issue to confront when discussing journalism in Latin America is fragmentation among a country's elite; for example, journalists, while well-informed about people in their own field, do not necessarily have contacts in such sectors as government or academia. Such fragmentation points to the need for interaction, whether electronically or in person, among experts from different fields or in the same field and from different countries.

Reinhard Keune raised the issue of whether journalists in one country of Latin America have an interest in what is going on in neighboring countries or continents. He cited a project eight years ago to create a region-wide TV network in ten Latin American countries; the project was never implemented because of lack of interest. Goodwin replied that he and Nacht found a good deal of interest among journalists in Latin America about the rapid changes taking place in other parts of the world, especially Europe. Nacht noted, however, that in general in Latin America there is a disdain for neighboring countries. Lisa Ellis described two Freedom Forum projects that have resulted in regional cooperation among journalists: a regional forum of newspaper publishers, in which individuals from 23 different countries meet to share ideas about solving problems; and an electronic network of approximately a dozen publishers' associations that features regular discussion groups.

Profession of Journalism:
Philip Arnold asked whether the concept of a vibrant, critical free press is accepted in Latin America. Michael Nacht said that it is difficult to generalize, given the huge differences between countries. In Chile, for example, newspapers are taken seriously but political realities prevent a truly vibrant press. In Mexico, while most newspapers reflect the government's priorities, there are some examples of a more independent press such as those dailies published by Alejandro Junco de la Vega.

Vivian Vahlberg brought up the issue of distance between owners/publishers and working journalists; for example owners often have networks of communications among themselves, but individual journalists do not. Michael Nacht replied that, in general, there is a gulf between the two, although there are exceptions.

Greg Adams asked about the issue of compensation among Latin American journalists, noting that in the United States journalists are well-paid and can therefore afford not to take bribes. He also asked whether CNN was admired in Latin America as a model, or seen as an intrusion. Michael Nacht replied that liberal intellectuals admire CNN, but those with more authoritarian impulses view the network with suspicion and as a threat.

Journalism Training Programs:
Andrea Taylor of the Ford Foundations suggested two elements to make journalism programs more effective: journalists involved should be associated with institutions at the heart of a country's policy making; and the exchange should be for a longer term. Michael Nacht cited the example of a Washington correspondent for a newspaper in Argentina who was deeply involved in Washington politics, but grew to be somewhat divorced from issues in his own country and region. Andrea Taylor asked if there could be some middle ground between that example and a short-term exchange. Peggy Blumenthal

responded by describing IIE's Tri-Lateral Journalist Exchange Program in which journalists from Canada, Mexico and the United States work with journalists in another North American country for three months while continuing to file with their home papers. This program has in some cases led to longer-term results through the establishment of foreign bureaus. Richard Krasno cited the example of the Friendly Press Fellowships, saying that it is important for journalists to be in another country long enough to get a feel for the issues, but not so long that they forget where they have come from.

Dan Heyduk raised the issue of motivation among Latin American journalists who come to the United States through training/exchange programs. He observed that we may think we are exposing them to a free press, while they may see the trip as an opportunity to gain access to contacts and practical skills; these two objectives do not always overlap. Craufurd Goodwin replied that while journalists are definitely interested in improving their skills, he and Nacht found a good deal of interest among Latin American journalists in observing the operation of the press in American society as well.

Victor Goldberg pointed out that the question underlying the issue of building a free press in Latin America hinges on who has the power to drive societal change. Journalists may have the desire to promote change, but not the power. The government is likely to feel threatened by change. The owners of the media may promote change, but only if they feel that they can do so safely. Various participants pointed out that the Inter-American Press Association, a gathering of owners, meets periodically and is considering how to open up Latin American societies in a cautious way.

On this point, Joan Dassin posed the following questions: What constitutes the demand for democracy in the countries of Latin America? What is the impetus for change? What mechanisms can be used to create a stronger demand for democracy? In what institutions, in which countries, in which social group would you provide incentives? What could be the logical fora for such discussions? How, over the long term, can you generate the institutional mechanism to keep debate in a society alive?

Conclusion
Craufurd Goodwin and Michael Nacht concluded the discussion by thanking the participants for their comments, and reiterating that the purpose of the meeting was to stimulate discussion on the value and role of U.S. training programs and U.S.—based institutions in strengthening the press in Latin America.

IIE RESEARCH SERIES

Additional single copies of this IIE Research Report can be ordered directly from IIE if accompanied by a check for $11 ($7 plus $4 for shipping). Orders should be directed to:

IIE Books, Institute of International Education
809 United Nations Plaza, New York, NY 10017-3580

Readers of this report may be interested in earlier titles in the series. They are available through the Educational Resources Information Center (ERIC). ERIC identificaton (ED) numbers are provided to assist in ordering. Call, fax, or write to the following address for price and order information:

EDRS/CBIS Federal Inc.
7420 Fullerton Road, Suite 110
Springfield, VA 22153-2852
Tel: 1-800-443-3742
Fax: 703-440-1408

Report 1
Absence of Decision:
Foreign Students in American Colleges and Universities
Carufurd D. Goodwin, Michael Nacht
(ED 232 492)

Report 2
Black Education in South Africa:
The Current Situation
David Smock

Report 3
A Survey of Policy Changes:
Foreign Students in Public Institutions of Higher Education
Elinor G. Barber
(ED 240 913)

Report 4
The ITT International Fellowship Program:
An Assessment After Ten Years
Marianthi Zikopoulos, Elinor G. Barber
(ED 245 635)

Report 5
Fondness and Frustration:
The Impact of American Higher Education on Foreign Students with
  Special Reference to the Case of Brazil
Craufurd D. Goodwin, Michael Nacht
(ED 246 710)

Report 6
International Expertise in American Business:
How to Learn to Play with the Kids on the Street
Stephen J. Kobrin
(ED 262 675)

Report 7
Foreign Student Flows:
Their Significance for American Higher Education
Elinor G. Barber, Editor
(ED 262 676)

Report 8
A Survey of Policy Changes:
Foreign Students in Public Institutions of Higher Education 1983–1985
William McCann, Jr.
(ED 272 045)

Report 9
Decline and Renewal:
Causes and Cures of Decay Among Foreign-Trained Intellectuals and
  Professionals in the Third World
Craufurd D. Goodwin, Michael Nacht
(ED 272 048)

Report 10
Choosing Schools From Afar:
The Selection of Colleges and Universities in the United States by Foreign
  Students
Marianthi Zikopoulos, Elinor G. Barber
(ED 272 082)

Report 11
The Economics of Foreign Students
Stephen P. Dresch
(ED 311 835)

Report 12
The Foreign Student Factor:
Their Impact on American Higher Education
Lewis C. Somon, Betty J. Young
(ED 311 836)

Report 13
International Exchange Off-Campus:
Foreign Students and Local Communiities
Mark Baldassare, Cheryl Katz
(ED 311 837)

Report 14
Mentors and Supervisors:
Doctoral Advising of Foreign and U.S. Graduate Students
Nathalie Friedman
(ED 295 541)

Report 15
Boon or Bane:
Foreign Graduate Students in U.S. Engineering Programs
Elinor G. Barber, Robert P. Morgan
(ED 295 542)

Report 16
U.S. Students Abroad:
Statistics on Study Abroad 1985/86
Marianthi Zikopoulos
(ED 295 559)

Report 17
Foreign Students in a Regional Economy:
A Method of Analysis and an Application
James R. Gale
(ED 331 404)

Report 18
Obligation or Opportunity:
Foreign Student Policy in Six Major Receiving Countries
Alice Chandler
(ED 312 981)

Report 19
Sponsorship and Leverage:
Sources of Support and Field of Study Decisions of Students from
    Developing Countries
Alan P. Wagner, Elinor G. Barber, Joanne King, Douglas M. Windham
(ED 331 405)

Report 20
Profiting from Education:
Japan–United States International Educational Ventures in the 1980s
Gail S. Chambers, William K. Cummings
(ED 320 488)

Report 21
Choosing Futures:
U.S. and Foreign Student Views of Graduate Engineering Education
Elinor G. Barber, Robert P. Morgan, William P. Darby
(ED 325 026)

Report 22
Daring to be Different:
The Choice of Nonconventional Fields of Study by International Women
    Students
Nelly P. Stromquist
(ED 332 633)

Report 23
Priming the Pump:
The Making of Foreign Area Experts
Jackson Janes
(ED 343 497)

Report 24
International Investment in Human Capital:
Overseas Education for Development
Craufurd D. Goodwin, Editor

Report 25
As Others See Us:
A Comparison of Japanese and American Fulbrighters
Eugene S. Uyeki
(ED 365 205)

Date Due

MCK DUE	NOV 15 2004	MCK RTD NOV 29 2004	
Mck DUE	APR 01 2005		